Power and
Empowerment

Peter Bachrach
AND
Aryeh Botwinick

Power and Empowerment

A Radical Theory of
Participatory Democracy

Temple University Press
PHILADELPHIA

Temple University Press, Philadelphia 19122
Copyright © 1992 by Temple University.
All rights reserved
Published 1992
Printed in the United States of America

The paper used in this publication meets
the minimum requirements of American
National Standard for Information Sciences
—Permanence of Paper for Printed Library
Materials, ANSI Z39.48-1984 ∞

Library of Congress
Cataloging-in-Publication Data
Bachrach, Peter.
    Power and empowerment : a radical
theory of participatory democracy / Peter
Bachrach and Aryeh Botwinick.
        p.   cm.
    Includes bibliographical references
and index.
    ISBN 0-87722-930-9 (cloth)
    ISBN 0-87722-939-2 (paper)
    1. Management—Employee
participation. I. Botwinick, Aryeh. II. Title.
HD5650.B138   1992
331'.01'12—dc20   91-32874

Page 42: Poem from *The Way of Life According
to Lau Tzu*, translated by Witter Bynner.
Copyright 1944 by Witter Bynner. Reprinted
by permission of HarperCollins Publishers.

For Adrienne
To the memory of Michael Oakeshott

Man would not have attained the possible unless time and again he had reached out for the impossible.

—MAX WEBER

Contents

Preface

Participatory democracy, a Rousseauian concept that reemerged during the intellectual turmoil of the 1960s, has been developed by social scientists in recent years into a full-blown theory of democracy. Although its focus is on the democratization of industry—according workers a significant role in decision making at all levels of a firm—its major importance is as a promising solution to the present decline and decay of American democracy.

The symptoms of the present crisis are well known. Almost half of the citizens no longer bother to vote. Elections have little relevance to major social and economic issues. The Democratic party seems to have lost its ability to mount an effective opposition in either leadership or philosophy in presidential elections.

Behind these symptoms is a less widely recognized disease afflicting much of American society. While wealth and power are increasingly concentrated in the upper classes and in the giant corporate oligarchies, the lower strata have suffered a depressed standard of living and a growing sense of powerlessness. The widening gap between the powerful few who rule and the alienated many who are ruled threatens the very existence of American democracy.

The objective of participatory democracy is thus not just to democratize the workplace for its own sake, but to have the workplace emerge as a point of leverage from which to achieve a more egalitarian redistribution of power, leading to a greater democratization of the entire political process.

If participation is to develop into an effective strategy for democratizing American society, it needs one ingredient that so far is sadly lacking: the support, legitimation, and guidance that social scientists could readily provide. Democratic theorists increasingly favor the democratization of industry, but they carefully avoid the problem of implementation. They limit their role to exploring what ought to be rather than including an examination of strategies of how to get "there" from "here." Social scientists who advocate workplace democracy have thus unwittingly helped relegate the democratization of corporate structures to a utopian plane.

The core of the problem is their refusal to contemplate democratic class struggle, despite its rich history in the United States and despite the *fact* that we are now experiencing intensely class-biased politics. By default, mainstream social scientists have handed the political right and Marxists exclusive rights to this key strategy for social change, ignoring the challenge to shape it as a useful democratic concept.

Some social scientists who see a role for class struggle in the cause of social reform often make the mistake of regarding it as a necessary evil. On the contrary, when a political struggle, initiated and mobilized from below, is conducted in accordance with democratic norms, it should be seen in a positive light, as an invaluable energizer of the system and as an effective counterforce to the power of money and status. Working-class struggle should thus be encouraged as a way of revitalizing our failing democratic polity by realigning political parties along class lines and expanding citizen participation and public awareness of issues of national concern. Americans' deeply ingrained fear of class politics—that is, class politics initiated *from below*—has prevented political thinkers from paying sufficient attention to the democratic value of this mode of political action.

It is highly ironic that in the midst of a democratic revolution in the communist world—a revolution in which American democracy in many respects serves as the model—we Americans languish in the face of our decaying democracy. We hope that the glare of this irony will spur social scientists to confront the American crisis of democracy with boldness and imagination. And we hope that our argument, both in its theoretical and ideological aspects, will serve as an additional spur. At minimum, we want to jolt our readers into seeing that (1) class politics is on the agenda whether they like it or not and (2) the categories of class and class struggle are now up for democratic redefinition in a way they have not been before in the twentieth century.

During the course of the last several years we have, either jointly or singly, presented various drafts of chapters of the book to several faculty and graduate seminars in universities and colleges and to panels of the American Political Science Association and the Northeastern Political Science Association meetings. The comments and criticisms made by our fellow political scientists at these sessions very much helped us to clarify and sharpen both the theoretical issues that we raised and those that we failed to raise.

We also want to thank the following individuals, who read the manuscript and provided criticisms and suggestions that were extremely helpful to us in completing the final version: Adrienne Bachrach, Marshall Berman, John Buell, Alfred Diamant, Richard Dudman, Barry Hoffmaster, Bruce Jennings, Kathy Lambert, Charles Moos, Frank Parkin, Eugene Schneider, Stephen White, and the anonymous readers at Temple University Press. Kathy Lambert has also benefited us greatly by providing the bibliography. We are indebted to Gloria Basmajian for her expert assistance in typing and retyping the manuscript. We are also grateful to Jane Cullen and Joan Vidal at Temple University Press and to Barbara Reitt for their encouragement and help in the various stages of the production of the book. Without Jane Cullen's prodding us to bring the book to fruition, it is doubtful that it would have seen the light of day.

Introduction

1

I

American workers in the 1990s are in a state of imminent demoralization and disarray. Economic recession, plant closings, unemployment, declining real wages, and overseas plant relocations have pushed the workers beyond ideology—into a preoccupation with their personal demands of making a living and making ends meet. In such a desperately shrinking and vanishing workplace, raising the banner of workplace democracy may seem cruelly ironic. However, our theory of participatory democracy as set forth herein is germane to the widespread anxiety of workers that has been generated by job insecurity. Our historical and theoretical argument for democratic class struggle, which we make in the book, is intended not only to enable workers to organize their work space more democratically than heretofore but also to provide them the decision-making leverage to obtain a substantial voice on key corporate issues, including the location of work.

The case for democratizing giant corporate oligarchies goes

beyond the issues of job security and democratic decision making in the workplace. It deals primarily with the issue of the decline and decay of American democracy. While wealth and power are increasingly concentrated in the upper classes and in the corporate structure, the lower strata suffer a depressed standard of living and a growing sense of powerlessness. As a result, a growing class division between the powerful few who rule and the alienated many who are ruled threatens the very existence of American democracy. We argue that participatory democracy provides a remedy for our political malaise. Furthermore, given imagination and boldness, we can put it into practice in full accordance with our democratic principles.

Democracy, defined from a liberal, mainstream perspective, "is a competitive political system in which competing leaders and organizations define the alternatives of public policy in such a way that the public can participate in the decision-making process."[1] In the workplace, participatory democracy is a political system in which all members of a firm, together with representatives of the community, participate equally in setting agendas and determining policy decisions for the firm. The engagement of workers and their allies in a struggle to democratize the workplace is the essential first step toward the restoration of a healthy polity, albeit still at this stage a liberal democratic society. The *process* of struggle to obtain the goal of participatory democracy in the workplace rivals in importance the goal itself. A sustained struggle of this kind constitutes the political ferment necessary to foster class politics and, in turn, the realignment of political parties and the emergence of national issues. Politics would once again become the concern of the people.

The ultimate aim is political transformation into a participatory society. In such a society the principle of participatory democracy is applied to all political groups, including government bureaucracies at all levels, factories and offices, universities, churches, business and trade associations, professional organizations, trade unions, and "private" clubs.

II

In 1977 Charles Lindblom concluded in his study *Politics and Markets*[2] that the dominance of corporate power in politics was a threat to American democracy. One of the key factors that concerned Lindblom was "the remarkable historical stability in the distribution of wealth and income—despite all the politics of the welfare state—in mature industrial societies." This, and other phenomena, reflect, he argued, "some of the most fundamental and pervasive features of industrial society" and can be explained largely by the overbearing influence of business in the determination of public policy.[3] Lindblom's theory was hardly new. Nevertheless, it had widespread influence, not only because it was persuasively argued but also because Lindblom for many years had been a leading proponent of the pluralist conception of American politics: that the political process was characterized by competition between many elites, not by the dominance of any one group. *Politics and Markets* represented a radical shift in position by arguing that the corporate sector was not to be characterized as an ordinary group, but one that is *sui generis* in its exercise of a preponderance of power.

Now, more than a decade later, the condition that Lindblom described—a growing disparity in the distribution of wealth and income in America—has worsened as the gulf between the rich and all other classes has continued to widen. The income gap between the richest one-fifth of families and the poorest one-fifth is now wider than at any time since the Bureau of Labor Statistics began keeping such records in 1949. The Congressional Budget Office estimates that the top 5 percent of American families will have, after accounting for inflation,

45 percent more in pretax income in 1990 than they did in 1980. This mammoth increase for the rich was enhanced by a drop of almost 10 percent in their taxes. Precisely the opposite trend occurred in the bottom of the income ladder. According to the budget office, the poorest 10 percent of American households will earn, in inflation-adjusted terms, 9 percent less in 1990 than they did in 1980. However, rather than paying 6.7 percent of their income in taxes as they did in 1980, they will pay 8.5 percent, an increase of almost 27 percent.[4]

The growing income gap between rich and poor can perhaps best be seen in demographic terms. The number of persons with family incomes under $15,000 in constant dollars expanded slightly between 1970 and 1985, while those with family incomes over $50,000—36 million of them—numbered roughly twice as many in 1988 as in 1983.[5] While the number of millionaires and their incomes soared and the number of people on the poverty level and below expanded in the 1980s, the bulk of the middle class remained at about the same level or declined, according to the Congressional Budget Office.[6]

The recent growth in the lopsided distribution of wealth has, as one would expect, exacerbated the maldistribution of power in the political arena. The radical change in federal income tax laws has been a prime factor in this development. Income tax rates sharply declined for upper-income households, from 70 percent in the top bracket in 1980 to 28 percent today. From a power perspective, it is most significant that the Democratic party—known traditionally as the party of the little man and of progressive tax rates—somehow felt it politically expedient to go along with this bonanza for the rich. "In accepting these 'reforms,'" writes Kevin Phillips, "Democrats not only voted for top rates contrary to their political traditions but lost the right to criticize tax policy as a source of both towering deficits and a concentration of wealth."[7]

The economic upsurge of the upper classes is also reflected in the way in which they have marshaled and used political power. They have been extremely effective, as Thomas Edsall points out, in organizing "grass-roots lobbying efforts, in the funding of conservative intellectual institutions, in the financing of a broad spectrum of political campaigns, in the formation of ad hoc legislative lobbying coalitions, in the political organization of stockholders and management-level personnel, and in de facto alliances with conservative ideological groups."[8]

The unprecedented increase in corporate power was also facilitated by the near collapse of corporate America's ideological and class rivals as the Democratic party simultaneously alienated two key groups from its historical constituency: white working people and black welfare recipients. White workers have defected in droves from a party that they identify with a welfare system that they regard as a device for diverting their hard-earned tax dollars to blacks. And the predominantly black underclass has become increasingly disenchanted by the party's inability to provide adequate housing, education, health services, and employment for the poor. Democratic cohesiveness has been further eroded by a wide breach between the better-off segments of the middle class, who are concerned with quality-of-life issues, and workers, whose focus is on job security.

The harshest blow to the power and status of the Democratic party, however, has been the dramatic decline of the trade-union movement in recent years. Labor unions no longer can serve as an effective power base of the party and thus as a primary constituency for the promotion of social democratic reforms. The percentage of American workers belonging to unions has fallen by more than half during the past quarter-century. In 1945 more than 35 percent of the workplace, excluding agriculture, was unionized. Today the figure is less than 17 percent. Owing to labor's precipitous decline and to encouragement from the Reagan and Bush administrations, employers have enjoyed an open season in union bashing. Illegal antiunion activities by companies have become common practice and are rarely penalized by a probusiness National Labor Relations Board. The board's antiunion bias is reflected by the statement of its chairman, Donald Dotson, that "collective bargaining means . . . the destruction of individual freedom."[9] And, as an editorial in the *New York Times* pointed out, "employers have recently perfected techniques to unravel existing contracts by first inviting strikes, and then replacing strikers with permanent hires."[10]

Paradoxically, the collapse of the union movement as both an economic and political force has not reduced public mistrust of unions. Public opinion polls consistently show that unions are seen as having "too much power." They are no longer seen, as they were forty years ago, as an essential institution of democracy, as a countervailing force to corporate power, and as a vehicle of empowerment for workers to voice their discontents and their challenge on the issue of goverance.

Finally, the disproportionate and increasing number of citizens with lower incomes who do not vote has significantly discouraged Democratic candidates and incumbents alike from taking progressive positions. Dukakis's refusal to be tarred by the "Big L" word says it all. His refusal was probably based on his awareness that the rich and near-rich—the top two quintiles of the electorate—comprised the largest bloc of people who actually vote and that it would be imprudent to antagonize these power holders. Like other politicians, he recognized the recent convergence of economic and electoral power. Not until it was too late did he challenge this power concentration by appealing, in effect, to people in the lower income strata to vote.

As long as American electoral campaigns continue to be waged along class-neutral lines, they will remain issueless, and as long as they remain issueless, they will undoubtedly expand the "nonparticipant party" of the lower classes and the consequent antidemocratic process.

III

In his 1981 presidential address to the American Political Science Association, Lindblom confronted the problem we have sketched out above, although in pessimistic terms. Attacking both incrementalism and revolution as inadequate theories of social change, Lindblom said, "We might then conclude that we are in prison in our existing institutions with no way out. That, I think, is a real possibility for even a long look at a foreseeable or guessable future. . . . Incrementalism never did in any case rule out the possibility of fundamental change through war or other causes and it may be true that our best, yet dismal, hope for structural change is through a transitory catastrophe."[11] But this approach reflects a bankruptcy of theory, which we are simply unprepared to countenance.

A less pessimistic scenario than Lindblom's relies on the inherent strength of the American political system to correct itself as it has in the past. It is argued that, as it becomes increasingly clear that the government is a captive of the rich, people become resentful and frustrated with their impotence in affecting public policy. This resentment will provoke what Kevin Phillips calls a watershed change in American politics. He likens the present period to two former periods of excess, the Gilded Age of the post–Civil War era and the 1920s. "In all three 'heydays' Republicans presided over boom cycles marked by conservative ideologies and probusiness governments, . . . periods in which the rich got richer and paid lower taxes." The first two of these periods of excess resulted in the Progressive Era and the New Deal. It is Phillips's thesis that the Republican excesses of the 1980s will induce another such reversal.[12] Phillips's prediction may well turn out to be true. Ironically, both presidents Reagan and Bush have exerted considerable energy to promote class politics: Reagan by his constant effort to dismantle the welfare state, and Bush by his commitment to enact a reduction in the capital gains tax and his refusal, during the budget crisis of 1990, to accept more than a symbolic increase in federal income taxes of the most wealthy Americans. What amounted to open declarations of class war by two Republican presidents, coupled with a devastating recession, may be sufficient to crystallize widespread resentment against the enormous concentration of wealth and its domination of American politics.

For all his optimism, however, Phillips ignores new political constraints that could stifle the political transformation that he envisages as comparable to the Progressive Era or the New Deal. Those transformations took place through the normal interplay of party politics. A new political transformation could hardly occur without the political mobilization of the working class and the incorporation of its demands by the Democratic party. Yet this scenario is called into question by a whole range of inhibiting factors. One of these is the persistence of a huge federal deficit. This burden of government debt is bound to keep in check the boldness and expansiveness required to launch, not to mention implement, any far-reaching progressive or reformist program. A second new political constraint is the remarkable expansion of the upper and upper-middle classes, which constitute a formidable electoral bloc, largely through their unrivaled capacity to reward with campaign contributions "deserving" politicians, whether Democratic or Republican. The inordinate political influence of this new political class will be the inevitable enemy of a democratic reform movement. With the shriveling of the trade unions, the Democratic party has little incentive to rely on them for an effective power base. Finally, the deep racial hostility of working-class whites toward the black underclass tends to make the Democratic party steer clear of its traditional liberal-oriented policies.

Even if Phillips's prediction were to come true, the coming of a second New Deal would not at this time be sufficient to revive an ailing American democracy. For a New Deal or a welfare-state strategy does not address the central problem that confronts American democracy—the maldistribution of economic and political power. Judging from both the American and European experience, the corporate power structure is essentially untouched by the welfare state. That is, corporate investment decisions, on which so much of society depends, are still made by corporate elites. If profit levels fall or if the executives lose confidence in the future, investment outlays may well be slashed. To avoid this possibility, government officials tend to shape public policy so as not to alarm business interests.[13] When they adopt welfare-state policies, officials accommodate citizens' wants in exchange for their electoral support. On its face this appears as a benign and equitable exchange. In reality, however, this trade-off consigns ordinary citizens to a position of powerlessness. And at the same time it leaves untouched the structural power of corporations. Citizens' demands are met only at the price of expanding bureaucratic control of the citizenry and thus deepening the institutionalization of inequality. In a word, the welfare strategy becomes part of the problem, not the solution.[14]

A more promising approach is embodied in our revised theory of participatory democracy, a theory, as will be seen, that, in sharp contrast to the welfare-state strategy, squarely attacks the two major problems that are responsible for the decline of American democracy: the maldistribution of power and the growing political alienation of most citizens. Moreover, the political struggle to implement the theory is itself likely to revitalize the democratic process. Finally, unlike the welfare-state strategy, its implementation would neither divide the races nor enlarge governmental bureaucracy. On the contrary, the success of a working-class movement in its struggle to achieve greater participatory rights in the workplace depends principally upon its ability to build worker solidarity as a source of power, rather than to rely on financial or political aid from government. A major advantage of the participatory strategy, in other words, is its independence from government. Its eventual relationship with government can be of a different order: As it gains a foothold in industry and greater power and voice in national politics, the participatory working-class movement can go forward to demand and achieve the democratization of the bureaucratic structure of government itself.

IV

As classically articulated by John Stuart Mill, the theory of democratic participation emphasizes the developmental and educational role that political participation plays in the cultivation of one's most fulfilled self. The individual is conceived as being in continual search of self-empowerment. Eventually, inquiry into and concern for the public good becomes the path to affirmation of a higher self. Carole Pateman echoes Mill's argument but underscores, perhaps more keenly than Mill himself, the dependence of self-development upon a continually nurturing context of social interaction. Hence she directs her animus against theorists of representative democracy for failing to appreciate the extent to which participation is integral to the process of personal growth and self-empowerment. Pateman seeks to institutionalize this insight in her participatory vision by maximizing participatory forums in society. She singles out the workplace in particular for participatory restructuring because it is where most ordinary people spend a major part of their waking lives. Their participation in workplace decision making thus becomes of critical importance in shaping a satisfactory life.[15] Contemporary radical democratic theorists have emphasized an additional dimension of political participation—that it affords excluded classes an opportunity to discover their real interests.[16] The underlying premise of participatory democracy—in contrast to liberal representative democracy—is that participatory democratic politics encompasses self-exploration and self-development by the citizenry. In sharp contrast, liberal doctrine conceives of democracy as merely facilitating passively the expression of *perceived* interests, not in helping citizens discover what their real interests are. As Samuel Bowles and Herbert Gintis sharply put it: "Liberalism claims that the marketplace and the ballot box allow people to get what they want. But liberalism is silent on how people might get to be what they want to be, and how they might get to want what they want to want." [17] Liberalism, in other words, assumes that individuals in the course of their private lives become fully aware of what constitutes their real political interests. Thus, given a reasonably representative political system, people are supposedly able to convert their wants into articulated political preferences.

In contrast to this key liberal assumption, participatory democratic theory points out that people from lower classes do not have the opportunity to acquire a political education in privatized socioeconomic and political institutions. To become conscious of their interests, they must actually become involved in the political process. If the process encourages democratic participation, it will be essentially educative. Through learning to communicate and reflect and engage in dialogue, and to act in concert with others, participants acquire the capacity to become reliably and realistically aware of what their political interests are.

The strong correlation between socioeconomic status and political participation is understandable in the light of this participatory premise. Since it is largely the lower classes who lack participatory structures to afford them an opportunity to help them determine who they are and what they want, it is not surprising that they primarily constitute the growing nonparticipatory party in American politics. It is this distribution that masks class structure in the United States. In the words of Walter Dean Burnham: "It is not far off the mark to conclude that there is greater class polarization these days between voters for either party and non-voters than between Democrats who vote and Republicans who vote."[18]

Democratic participation enables participants to gain a better understanding of their real interests and thereby furthers the democratic objective of equality. The interdependence between democratic participation and equality of sharing in political power is the crux of participatory democracy. Equality of power is rooted in the democratic belief in moral equality, and both ideals together rest on the imperative that ordinary citizens must play an important role in shaping their individual and collective destinies. Equality is also rooted in a growing skepticism that undermines the legitimacy of elites putting forward moral and political claims based upon privileged sources of knowledge. As Amy Gutmann puts it: "By opening up opportunities for free and equal participation in political life (broadly understood), an equalitarian society gives credence to the ideal of equal moral persons upon which it is theoretically based."[19]

The connection between participation and equality brings into bold relief an important aspect of participatory politics. This type of politics has the potential for reordering American politics so that, instead of being concerned with influencing the relatively insignificant moves that are made within the existing rules of the game, it can call into question the rules themselves. The objective of participatory democracy is thus not just to democratize the workplace for its own sake, but to have the workplace emerge as a point of leverage from which to achieve a more egalitarian redistribution of power, leading to a greater democratization of the entire political process.

In the short run, the aim of the democratization of industry is threefold: The first is to spur the mobilization of workers and their allies to engage in class struggle for expanded participatory rights. A struggle of this kind, we argue, is the most effective strategy at this time to restore the health of the political process. The second is to diminish the political domination of corporate elites. The third is to create political space for the underclasses to acquire voice and a more empowered sense of community involvement, thereby enabling them to compete more effectively with the upper classes in all arenas of politics. Today the more affluent groups in American society have abundant opportunities to participate in both the public and private sectors. These opportunities allow them to accumulate knowledge and cultivate political skills that nurture the confidence and the ability they need to assert themselves effectively. Expanded and newly created participatory counterstructures are therefore essential if the subordinate classes are to develop sufficient social consciousness and political skills to effectively articulate and defend their interests. We describe both of these aims—the devolution of corporate decision making and the politicization of working people—as important steps toward the revitalization and expansion of political democracy.

Although the workplace is the crucial setting for reforming the American political system, workers are not the only group that must address these issues of greater equalization of power. Environmentalists, feminists, neighborhood and civil rights activists are also vital to this struggle, especially as they join hands with workers in forging a coalition around issues of common interest.[20] Environmentalists in alliance with workers, for example, will be more effective politically in opposing industrial pollution, whether in the workplace or in the community at large, than environmentalists pursuing these goals by themselves. Similarly, workers, feminists, neighborhood, and civil rights groups stand to gain by collaborating on such issues as housing, education, child care, health benefits, and the minimum wage. Since the overwhelming majority of members in such groups are subordinate salary and wage earners, they share a potential common interest in the promotion of workplace democracy.

V

Chapter 2 comprises a critical analysis of the theory of participatory democracy. We present the basic arguments made by liberal theorists against participatory theory during the past several years as forcefully as we can. In the course of formulating counterarguments against this liberal offensive, we have found it necessary to revise participatory theory to some extent. In its reconstructed form we think it is a sound theory, responsive to the strong evidence that American democracy is in trouble.

What role can theory play toward activating large numbers of workers and their leaders in a struggle to extend citizens' participatory rights as a means of achieving economic democracy? In confronting this question (which we introduce in Chapter 3) the theorist must face up to a formidable irony of the political system: On the one hand, it constitutionally guarantees a whole range of rights to facilitate citizen participation in the public arena, and, on the other, it fosters a mobilization of bias, which operates effectively to curtail widespread citizen participation, especially among those from the lower classes. To the progressive strategist, the irony presents a difficult dilemma: Mass participation from below can effectively combat the mobilization of bias, but, at the same time, the mobilization of bias is an effective constraint against the growth of widespread participation.

This dilemma, which can be expressed as a tension between established power structures and citizen empowerment, is central to our study. The "mobilization of bias"[21] refers to a set of structures including norms, beliefs, rituals, institutions, organizations, and procedures ("rules of the game") that operate systematically to benefit certain groups and persons at the expense of others. Normally it is most effective in preventing issues potentially dangerous to the defenders of the status quo from reaching the decision-making agenda. Its effectiveness is primarily measured by its ability to maintain citizen political passivity. The large and expanding party of nonparticipants in politics is a mark of its presence today. In effect, we conclude that the system, the rules of the game, consists in the mobilization of bias. Thus, the primary challenge of proponents of participatory democracy is to change, to democratize, the rules. That is, contrary to mainstream social scientists who favor workplace democracy, we argue that this kind of reform cannot be accommodated within the present political system, that the system itself must be changed in the course of class struggle to achieve workplace democracy. However, we shall also argue that the calling into question of traditional democratic rules of the game itself constitutes a well-defined and influential countertradition in American political history—so that the American way of doing politics consists in periodically raising for public scrutiny the ground rules of democratic policy formation and institution building themselves.

Chapters 4 and 5 summarize the progress that has been made toward establishing workplace democracy in western Europe and the United States. Some time ago Philip Selznick observed that "participatory democracy" performs a cooptative function by giving "the opposition the illusion of a voice without the voice itself, and so stifles opposition without having to alter policy in the least."[22] His observation, made thirty-five years ago, is not far off the mark when applied to today's power relations between management and labor. Despite the growth of participatory structures in the workplace—especially in European countries—management remains the dominant force in determining economic policy. Corporate power, however, is not the only barrier to the democratization of the economy. Another barrier is the trade unions. Although they have played a crucial role in the development of worker participatory structures on the continent, unions have persistently usurped power within these structures, thus replacing corporate control with union control. In America their role has been substantially different. They have been a barrier to workplace democracy because of their reluctance, if not timidity, to fight for it. They refuse to see that objective forces at work in the economy have increasingly linked advanced technology with worker participation, that, despite the resistance of management, new technology requires the creative input of workers in decision making in areas of production, service, and administration. Indeed, without a strong commitment by organized labor to lead a struggle for workplace democracy, its very survival as a labor movement may be thrown into doubt.

Trade-union leaders are not the only group on the left to have waffled on the issue of workplace democracy. Democratic theorists increasingly favor the democratization of industry, but they assiduously avoid the problem of implementation. They seem to limit their role as social theorists to exploring issues of what ought to be, not to considering strategies of how to get "there" from "here." As a result, as we argue in Chapter 6, social scientist proponents of workplace democracy have unwittingly contributed to relegating the issue of the democratization of corporate structures to a utopian plane.

The last three chapters are concerned with strategies we believe essential to promote, in Gramsci's terms, counterhegemonic forces, leading to a political struggle centered on the issue of workplace democracy. In Chapter 7 we argue that the existing division of society between the private and public spheres—a structural division that safeguards liberal capitalism—must be radically altered. Public space must be enlarged to encompass large corporations and thereby strip away their legitimacy, as private institutions, to rule autocratically. For these future public institutions, such as the large corporations, democracy must become the rule. However, the expansion of the public space should not be extended to the point that it endangers private space, which is essential to nurture new and unorthodox ideas and ways of life. In Chapter 8, we formulate a democratic concept of class struggle through an analysis and comparison of our notion of the concept with that of James

Madison and the classical Marxists. We argue on both historical and theoretical grounds that class struggle, when initiated by subordinate groups and classes to expand their democratic rights, should be seen as a justified and often an indispensable democratic strategy. We emphasize that democratic class struggle should not be viewed as a necessary evil in the cause of social reform. On the contrary, it should be welcomed and encouraged as a way to revitalize our failing democratic polity, as a way to realign parties along class lines and thus generate expanded citizen participation and public consciousness of issues of national concern. Americans' deeply ingrained fear of class politics has prevented American political thinkers from paying sufficient attention to the contributions that class politics could make within a mature liberal constitutional system.

In Chapter 9 we focus on the key questions of what motivates the extreme political passivity of American workers at this time and what strategy appears most likely to overcome this passivity. Worker political passivity, we argue, results from the effectiveness of the existing mobilization of bias. It is not only that workers have been manipulated by a cultural hegemony and therefore embrace establishment values. Although this is partly so, their passivity stems primarily from their lack of an alternative philosophy and program that makes sense to them in terms of their actual experience. The mobilization of bias plays a crucial role in this process, not by dictating values that workers should embrace, but rather by *not* providing the necessary conditions and political climate for workers to evolve an alternative position of their own.

Political theorists can most effectively contribute to the creation of an alternative vision by telling working men and women themselves in plain language that as free people in a democratic society they should have the right to participate in making decisions in the workplace that affect their lives; that their exercise of this right is crucial to the diminution of their deep sense of anxiety and powerlessness; and that their exer cise of this right would significantly strengthen and invigorate American democracy as a whole.

Workers and their allies, including progressive political theorists, must come to see this right as something worth fighting for in a new class struggle that is fully within the accepted tradition of American democracy.

A Critical Analysis and Reconstruction of Participatory Theory

2

The development of a contemporary theory of participatory democracy—and, more narrowly, of workplace democracy—has posed a direct challenge to the basic principles and underlying assumptions of liberal democracy. We consider liberal democratic conceptions of human nature as static and deficient, and liberal democratic conceptions of politics, equality, and democracy as excessively narrow and elitist oriented.

In response to attacks by participatory theorists, liberal democrats have engaged in a critical comparison of the principal concepts underlying the two theories of democracy in efforts to buttress their own case for liberal democracy. The burden of the liberal defense has been that if participatory theory were actually implemented, it would be disastrous, fostering political inequality, excessive political fragmentation, narrow-mindedness, an erosion of individual freedom, and ineffectual leadership. These are serious charges and warrant an equally serious examination.

I

Liberal democracy consists largely of a representative system in which law and public policy are made by officeholders who have won freely contested elections. In the words of George Kateb, "the electoral system is a form of people's self-rule."[1] However, this is true only to the extent that officeholders respond to popular needs and interests and are held periodically accountable to the people's judgment of their performance. The system is founded upon the assumption that citizens are aware of their self-interest and are able to pursue it through their vote.

As we have seen, participatory theorists regard the liberal conception of democracy as fundamentally flawed because it fails to recognize political participation as an essential value in itself, necessary to the growth and full development of all citizens. According to this view, a democratic polity has the obligation of meeting not only the material and social welfare interests and needs of its citizens—which representative democracy focuses upon—but also of providing political conditions to facilitate maximum self-development, conditions that will provide all individuals with an opportunity "to enlarge their vision and sense of themselves."[2] Along the same lines, the late C. B. Macpherson argued that democracy must be "seen as a kind of society, not merely a mechanism of choosing and authorizing governments. . . . The egalitarian principle inherent in democracy requires not only 'one man, one vote,' but also 'one man, one equal effective right to live as fully humanly as he may wish'. . . . This principle requires . . . a concept of man as at least potentially a doer, an exerter and developer and enjoyer of his human capacities, rather than merely a consumer of utilities."[3]

The key concept in participatory theory, maximum self-development, derives from the proposition that ordinary people have the capacity to develop not only their internal selves but also a potential for expanding their self-interest to encompass an identification with and a commitment to the well-being of others. However, from Rousseau onward, the concept of self-development has been criticized most tellingly on grounds of ambiguity and fuzziness. How can maximum self-development be recognized or measured? Political theorist John Dunn claims that "the idea of maximizing a value which is not in any way measurable, or even linear, is a notion which wears an air of slightly bogus imprecision at the best of times."[4] He wants to know what human capacities should be maximized and what constitute the criteria to determine their maximization? In criticizing C. B. Macpherson's theory of self-developmental democracy, Steven Lukes likewise points out that the human capacities or powers to be developed "rely for their specification upon an abstract, individualist ethical perfectionism, not yet spelled out." Moreover, "the impediments to their use and development remain indeterminate, so long as those capacities and the forms of social life which both enable and constitute their realization remain unspecified."[5]

The goal of maximizing self-development has been attacked not only because it is hopelessly vague, but also because it is utopian. It is considered utopian because it would require for its realization an egalitarian society not dominated by acquisitive values, before it could validly serve as a guiding principle for action, much less be actualized or even approximated.

II

Perhaps the most telling rejoinders to the participatory argument are the findings of multiple surveys and empirical studies that tend to undermine the democratic faith in the good character and reasonableness of ordinary citizens. These studies repeatedly conclude that the American masses are politically passive and poorly informed about public affairs and politics. Worse still, they have a disturbingly weak commitment to the core democratic values of freedom of speech and religion, dignity of the individual, and due process of law. However, it has been consistently found that the upper social classes exhibited a significantly greater support for tolerance and democracy than do the working and poorer classes.[6] In light of these findings, some theorists argue that the focus should be on protecting liberal values from the excesses of democracy rather than, as we argue, upon the need to expand democracy.[7]

A widespread public commitment to the fundamental norms underlying the democratic process was regarded by classical democratic theorists as essential to the survival of democracy. Today social scientists tend to reject this position. They do so not only because of their limited confidence in the commitment of nonelites to freedom, but also because of the growing awareness that nonelites are, in large part, politically activated by elites. The empirical findings that mass behavior is generally instigated in response to the attitudes, proposals, and modes of action of political elites gives added support to the position that maintaining the rules of the game does not depend upon the people but upon an elite.[8]

In their influential and widely adopted political science textbook, Thomas Dye and Harmon Zeigler state, "Democracy is government 'by the people', but the survival of democracy rests on the shoulders of elites. This is the irony of democracy: Elites must govern wisely if government 'by the people' is to survive."[9] Unlike the Founding Fathers, their fear is not that the people greedily covet the property of the rich, but rather that they have cultivated a deep-seated disregard, if not contempt, for democracy. The masses, in their view, are "authoritarian, intolerant, anti-intellectual, nativistic, alienated, hateful, and violent." Dye and Zeigler fully recognize that elites are capable of taking repressive action, but this occurs only when elites feel threatened by mass unrest.[10] The masses pose a fundamental threat to democracy because they are prone either to take direct action against democratic institutions and values, or provoke counterelites to engage in antidemocratic action. The survival of democracy therefore depends, they argue, upon the leadership of "an enlightened elite" to shape and direct policy aimed principally to keep the masses politically quiescent. This strategy is surely diametrically opposed to encouraging widespread political participation from below, as favored by proponents of participatory democracy.

III

The theory of democratic participation is based upon the assumption that there is a close linkage between participation and equality. Some liberal theorists in taking their stand against participationists have argued that exactly the opposite is true, that participation fosters inequality. For example, J. R. Lucas writes: "Any system that calls for more than minimal participation will favor the active over the apathetic and the rich over the poor. . . . Participation is inegalitarian." [11] This conclusion is well supported by numerous investigations throughout the world on the relationship between social class and participation. "No matter how class is measured, the studies consistently show that higher-class persons are more likely to participate in politics than lower-class persons." [12] This phenomenon also prevails, even when the decision-making process is expressly designed to conform to the norms of participatory democracy. In Yugoslavia, for example, factory council managers and skilled workers are the dominant decision makers. The unskilled remain largely silent. [13] In New York City and other urban centers in the United States, community control of schools further supports findings that participatory democracy has become an effective vehicle for the domination of the educated over the uneducated. Adherents of the United Federation of Teachers "had little trouble taking control of many local school districts in New York City, given the 'participation gap' between their constituencies and those of candidates representing a poorer, less-educated population."[14] Verba and Nie cite evidence that "group consciousness" among the poor can help close this participation gap, but there is also evidence that the gap has been further widened by the rise of group consciousness among whites in communities where desegregation is a hotly contested issue.[15]

On the basis of her review of the literature on community control of schools, Gutmann pessimistically concludes that the "participatory ideal behind community control itself presupposes . . . relative equality of income and educational opportunities. . . . Without these equalities, community control may lead to greater participatory inequalities and perhaps even to more substantive inequalities between advantaged and disadvantaged groups."[16] In her superb work *The New American Dilemma* Jennifer Hochschild concurs: "Citizen participation exacerbates existing inequalities between minorities and whites. . . . We are dealing here with a vision that is normatively very powerful but empirically very seldom realized."[17]

Further, critics argue that a truly democratized participatory system would tend to evolve into a highly fractionalized, directionless society composed of a multiplicity of participatory groups, each driven primarily by parochial and selfish interests.[18] They envisage the possibility of larger, technologically advanced, and powerful "democratically" controlled enterprises leaving the less successful industrial groups—the smaller, labor-intense, and less technologically advanced firms, together with the growing underclass—vulnerable to their domination. There is nothing in participatory theory or practice to preclude the state from becoming unduly receptive to the special interests of powerful industrial organizations, however much worker controlled they might be. In short, the critics point out, there is no reason to suppose that worker-controlled industries would diminish the greed and selfishness of industrial decision makers, whether they are called workers or business people.

Participatory theory has also been criticized for focusing on the interrelationship among individuals within distinct collectives, thereby ignoring the broader needs of society as a whole and implicitly mandating that each collective regard the organization as "theirs," and that its members, rather than outsiders, constitute the authoritative source of decision making.[19] Thus, even though collectives would be called "public" in the nomenclature of participatory theory, in reality each collective would be regarded as the private turf of those who controlled it.

In view of participatory theorists' reliance on Rousseau, critics find it puzzling that participationists have not recognized the potentially dangerous impact that "public enterprises" conceived in a participatory vein could have on the quality of national politics. "We face a choice," Barnard and Vernon write, "between reinforcing partial attachments and effacing the public, and reinforcing the public and effacing partial attachments; but participationists show a pronounced tendency to attempt both at once, as though the general will of partial and general associations were somehow complementary to each other."[20]

Participationists have also been attacked for embracing the Rousseauian concept of a small-group society, striving to achieve social and economic equality between its members, on the grounds that it nurtures oppressive uniformity. George Kateb writes: "The political procedures and arrangements of direct democracy in its most modern form . . . requires a social and economic context that wars on psychological and spiritual complexity, on the extensions and display of human facilities, on the illimitable annexations of human experience."[21] Democracy of this nature, he argues, makes "any impulse to dissent into an act of shameful rebellion against oneself, of shameful inconsistency." For Kateb, direct democracy is the end of individualism and does away with the chance to gain autonomy. To the question of whether there is a plausible alternative to direct democracy that escapes Rousseauian oppressiveness, his answer is a resounding "No." [22]

IV

The alleged weaknesses in the theory of participatory democracy—that it is vague and utopian, fostering inequality, conformity, and parochial and selfish attitudes toward politics—are, according to liberal theorists, avoided in representative democracy. In fact, they insist that a representative system tends to combat these characteristics, in three important ways.

First, a representative system is rooted in the egalitarian concept of universal suffrage. Differences among people, owing to inequalities in education, income, and political skills, which are so readily manifest in a participatory politics, are democratically filtered when the principle of one person, one vote is practiced. This principle, the liberal democrat is quick to emphasize, favors the mass, the disadvantaged, the inarticulate, and the politically withdrawn, not the elite.[23] Jack Nagel writes: "Egalitarian democrats must assign ultimate legitimacy to those methods that encourage the most extensive participation. . . . [They should] heed plenary assemblies rather than committees, ballots rather than long meetings, and elected representatives rather than self-selected activists."[24]

Second, it is argued, representative democracy is to a large extent an effective antidote to the selfish, parochial interests exacerbated by decentralized, participatory forms of decision making. Following the theoretical lead of James Madison, liberals hold that a large representative system provides necessary space between the particular interests of particular persons and the interests of the whole to enable legislators to resolve conflicting claims in a reasonably rational and public-spirited way.[25]

Third, it is alleged that the democratic system of representation, despite its defects, promotes individual freedom and morality. It is moderated by moral considerations largely because "political authority is chastened by the electoral system."[26] Contested free elections serve the invaluable democratic purpose of keeping officeholders "honest" and promoting an "independence of spirit" among ordinary people. Furthermore, representative democracy, as perceived by Kateb, "is committed to respecting the boundaries of the individual, and the related separation of society and the state; yet it establishes a mutual moral permeability between public and nonpublic. In contrast, direct democracy effaces boundaries and separations, while subjecting everything to the publicly political imperative. This imperative repels the exploration of possibilities in public life that the spirit of representative democracy fosters."[27]

Kateb's case for representative institutions, in contrast to participatory democracy, is extendable to the theory and practice of leadership in liberal society. After all, the political representative in a legislative setting functions as a quasi-leader—placing his or her personal stamp on the plethora of heterogeneous interests being pursued by constituents. Liberal theorists have argued that effective democratic leadership in the executive sphere correspondingly requires a certain amount of citizen passivity. A politically active citizenry deprives leaders of slack resources necessary for creative and imaginative leadership[28] and leads to a dangerous overload of the political system.[29] It would appear that the government is presently "overloaded" since, in the face of the huge federal deficit, it is unable to act effectively in meeting the needs of the people. In his well-known analysis of the "overload," Samuel Huntington argues that excessive demands from the citizenry and democracy itself are the primary causes of this phenomenon. He claims that the "democratic surge" of the 1960s, reflected in massive increases in government spending in public welfare, education, social security, health, and hospitals, raised the level of mass expectations, which in turn— as government was unable to meet these expectations—set the stage for a sharp decline in authority. The gulf between popular expectations for governmental services and governmental capacity has led to what he calls a "distemper of American politics." To avoid "overload," the "democratic political system requires some measure of apathy and noninvolvement on the part of some individuals or groups."[30] In effect, what is needed, he argues, is less rather than more democracy.

V

In the face of the liberal counterattack, must we concede that the case for participatory democracy is irredeemably flawed? We do not believe so. Before we present our case for participatory democracy, it is important to recognize that the liberal critique addresses this concept as exemplified within ongoing enterprises—for example, worker ownership of companies, community control of schools, neighborhood management of integrated housing—rather than focusing upon a more radical embodiment of the participatory ideal, namely, the democratization of industry conceived in macro and class terms. Since our main concern centers upon the democratic feasibility of a transformation of power in the political arena and in society as a whole, from oligarchical to democratic rule, our theoretical orientation is considerably broader than if our objective were limited to justifying the democratization of industry.

At the outset, we partially concur with the liberal criticism that the concept of "maximum self-development" as a distinguishable and independent political ideal is excessively vague and amorphous. The meaning of "maximization" gets diluted given the complexities of the human condition and the wide differences in disposition, attitude, values, and outlook among individuals. Moreover, the participationists must know that the participatory experience can have a psychologically dysfunctional effect, since it can feed the egocentric traits of some and demean others who feel shy and inadequate. Finally, we cannot lose sight of those whose self-esteem is enhanced precisely by their systematic rejection of democratic values in their struggle for personal gain and power.

However, in our view, these potential limitations do not undermine the basic participatory assumption, that democratic participatory experience usually fosters participants' self-development and promotes communal values. To be more precise, democratic participation with others can be expected to lead to revised understandings of the participants' capacities and resources, leading in turn to new conceptualizations of their individual and collective self-interest. "Self-development" in this sense does not connote the pursuit of statically defined interests but underscores the cultivation of new insights into a continually expanding image of self—which leads to the articulation of new notions of self-interest. In the context of participatory theory, self-development connotes the process by which persons gain through dialogue and interaction with others a sense of personal identity linked with augmented clarity concerning their interests and combined with an enhanced recognition of others. "Process," of course, suggests not a one-shot affair but a continuing network of interaction with others, which highlights the primacy of process for making sense of one's life in community. Therefore, the best antidote to the shortcomings of participation is still more participation. The process-character of participation has a built-in safeguard since it encourages a continuing reassessment of previous outcomes. Moreover, it facilitates actions that would be inconceivable in the absence of interaction with others. A third facet of "process" is its close linkage with power. The individual's transition from relative powerlessness to one of power when he or she becomes part of a participatory network facilitates an invaluable registering of the dynamics of power. The sharing of power with others in a participatory setting paradoxically yields an augmentation of the power of the self as well as an enhancement of the power of the group of which one is a part. When one takes one's destiny into one's own hands through participatory involvement with others, both the power of the individual and of the group are often increased, which leads to a sense of solidarity and individual well-being.

There is substantial empirical evidence that political participation does nurture and heighten group identity; in sharpening awareness of the individual self, it can also engender a transformation from a sense of powerlessness to power. The civil rights and women's movements have demonstrated the remarkable capacity of a mass movement—by fomenting continuous dialogue and struggle—to reshape an amorphous and passive mass into a cohesive group of highly articulate, politically aware actors. These movements also demonstrated how, in the course of struggle, members deepened their understanding of the issues. The civil rights movement, for example, which initially focused on Negro segregation on buses and at lunch counters, soon spread to encompass the struggle of blacks against the class problem of poverty. Women, who began with a demand for equal treatment in the man's world, soon shifted to challenging the values of that world. In both groups participation led to a new sense of self: for the first time, participants in both groups belonged; they felt a heady sense of power.

Workers who take up the struggle for workplace democracy could be expected to experience a comparable enlargement as a result of participatory politics. As they gain experience in the democratic process, workers acquire an appreciation of democracy in the context of their own lives. By taking part in the democratic process, workers, like blacks and women before them, may also acquire enough of a sense of political efficacy to prompt their taking an active part in local and national politics.

In sum, we recognize that maximum self-development is excessively vague and utopian. This does not diminish in any respect the centrality of the concept of self-development in the theory of participatory democracy. However, in this theory it is important to distinguish between two separate conceptions of self-development. In the first, self-development ties in with the traits fostering "possessive individualism"—an augmentation, through a heightened self-image, of capacities and potentialities favoring egotism. In the second conceptualization, self-development leads to the cultivation of a sense of full being as predicated upon others' sense of full being—the recognition that the traits and powers that define our humanity are sum-sum rather than zero-sum in character.

We acknowledge the importance of what the existing literature stresses, that participation facilitates individuals' discovering who they are and what they want. However, from our perspective, self-development also emphasizes the interdependence between self-empowerment and group empowerment. Within the context of an acquisitive society these conceptions, as we shall see in Chapter 6, tend to be in conflict since the societal norm of acquisitiveness favors the development of egocentric traits. However, in periods of social strife, when workers are engaged in collective action against employers, their sense of solidarity and group empowerment is nurtured and developed. We argue that, viewed from an institutional perspective, working-class struggle can be a democratic force in realigning political parties, combating political fragmentation, stimulating political participation, and fostering the reemergence of important national issues during electoral campaigns. We now want to add that working-class struggle can contribute to democracy in another important way: by nurturing democratic attitudes and values in working men and women, including a sense of group empowerment, and concurrently engendering a growing awareness and understanding that the idea of democracy is more than an abstraction, that it can play an important role in the improvement of the quality of life for working people and their communities. An advantage of workplace democracy as a political issue is that once it is accepted on the political agenda it will necessitate a long struggle for it to be realized. A prolonged struggle over this issue will provide an opportunity for workers to gain a political education and for the forces of institutional democratic reform to gain a foothold in American political life.

VI

Perhaps the most disturbing counterargument against the theory of participatory democracy is that mass political quiescence is essential to the stability and health of democracy. In our judgment, widespread mass participation is an indispensable component of a healthy democratic polity. In its absence, leaders become unresponsive to the needs of the people. As the power gap between ruler and ruled increases, the masses can become alienated, disaffected, and mean, and in so becoming, render democracy vulnerable to attack by an antidemocratic mass movement. More importantly, a "democracy" that condones, or even promotes, widespread mass nonparticipation denies large strata of the population the multiple benefits derived from political participation—and thus undermines its principal reason for being, namely, to promote the well-being of all the people.

The illiberal and, indeed, antidemocratic propensity of ordinary men and women is an undeniable fact that must be confronted. To face it realistically, however, does not mean, as most critics of participation assume, that the undemocratic beliefs and attitudes of the masses are immutable. In a statement that seems to cast doubt upon the validity of this assumption, Dye and Zeigler write: "Lacking a sense of purpose or responsibility or community identification, the individual in the mass becomes isolated, atomized, and alienated. In contrast, when individuals are involved in their family, their union, or other social groups, their neighborhood or city, they can develop a sense of purpose, responsibility, and personal effectiveness. *Moreover, if the masses are involved with such concerns, they are unavailable for mass political activity*" (italics supplied).[31]

If people can be psychologically enriched and disciplined by becoming actively engaged in nonpolitical pursuits, as Dye and Zeigler claim, then why stop at nonpolitical involvement? Following their line of reasoning, should we not expect that a considerable number of average men and women would discard their antidemocratic attitudes as they became involved in participatory politics and thus acquired a stake in democracy? Of course this strategy involves the risk that the masses, driven by their initial antidemocratic beliefs, would exercise their newfound freedom for antidemocratic ends before they acquired a political education in democracy. On the other hand, if the risk of democratization is considered too great, will not the existing democratic-elitist system be chronically exposed to attack from mass-supported demagoguery? To face the risk realistically does not require us to rely upon elites to sustain the system. Democratic elitism is preserved at a heavy price. It saps democracy of the boldness and imaginativeness we expect of it. For the system, rooted in mobilization of bias that is designed to perpetuate mass political passivity, will continue to exclude a whole range of issues that might otherwise challenge existing power structures. And in doing so, it will continue to deprive a substantial majority of people of the rich and rewarding political life that the minority enjoy.

A more courageous and rewarding strategy would be to encourage the working class and their allies to mount an organized struggle to democratize industry. A strategy of this nature would, to quote Dye and Zeigler, "develop a sense of purpose, responsibility, and personal effectiveness" among a large mass of individuals who have become "isolated, atomized, and alienated."[32]

VII

In contradistinction to the liberal view that participation promotes inequality, the radical version of participatory democracy emphasizes the ways in which participation and equality are mutually reinforcing. Liberals make a telling point that racially and economically integrated participatory groups tend to exacerbate inequalities between rich and poor, educated and uneducated. They are wrong to conclude, however, as Gutmann does, that "relative equality of primary-good distribution is a prerequisite of equality of participation."[33] Making economic equality a prerequisite for democratic participation depoliticizes participation and relegates it to a utopian status.

Although inequality tends to be fostered within isolated participatory groups in a capitalist society, this does not mean that the same result would occur within a class-oriented participatory movement. A participatory organizational strategy that is predicated upon class cleavage is likely to generate worker solidarity and yields psychological space for lower-strata workers to acquire both an interest and a competence in politics. In the context of class conflict, political involvement becomes contagious even to the shy and inarticulate. And to the extent that such a strategy to gain a participatory foothold in industry is successful, the power and status gap between capital and labor is narrowed. Success of this sort is indicative of the theoretically and practically permeable relationship that subsists among democratic participation, power, and equality. Participation, as a manifestation of power, generates greater equality

between classes, which in turn serves as an ideological catalyst for subordinate classes to struggle for their equal rights
to participate. Also, as we will argue, the idea of democratic
leadership that is integral to the theory of participatory democracy serves as a spur to workers on the lower levels within the
workforce to participate.

The multiple linkages that prevail among democratic participation, power, and equality are central to the realization
of the twofold nature of the participatory ideal: the struggle
for equality in decision making in industry and the continual
concern to diminish inequalities within the participatory movement itself. Connecting participation not merely with self-
development but with fairer distributions of power within society as a whole fosters acknowledgment of the open-endedness
of the participatory ideal. Admittedly, new power groupings—
even participatory ones—engender their own intragroup inequalities. However, making equalization of power central
to democratic participation enables members of newly empowered participatory groups to insist upon greater equalization of power within the protest groups themselves. In other
words, our conceptualization of the relationship among participation, power, and equality suggests that the corrective to
the degenerative dynamics of participation—that it engenders
inequalities of its own—lies in participation itself.

In summary, our argument that political participation can
promote equality in an inegalitarian society holds that: (1) The
initial impact of participation is to generate inequality among
participants. (2) However, in a macro and class context, workers' struggles to gain participatory rights in industry can
serve as an effective instrumentality for engendering on a
macro level greater equality between classes. (3) The emerging
contradiction between the external success of a worker participatory movement's struggle against management and internal
inequalities among the workers within the movement has the
potential of motivating relatively subordinate members to de-

mand their rights within the participatory movement itself. This dialectic was exemplified in the recent history of Solidarity. The success of Solidarity vis-à-vis the Communist party in Poland demonstrated to subordinate elements within the movement the contradiction between their external triumph and their failure to be consulted and actively involved in the decision-making process of the movement.

VIII

To turn to another line of liberal criticism of participatory democracy introduced earlier: is it not likely that workers will utilize their newfound decision-making power in industry to satisfy their own parochial and selfish interests? Why should it be assumed that working-class power, unlike other forms of power, will bind itself to democratic principles and norms?

We believe that this danger of engendering a possessive individualist mentality among workers embroiled in a battle for participatory rights is not likely to occur for a number of reasons. First, it is extremely doubtful that the establishment of widespread participatory rights for workers in industry would be tolerated by the community at large without effective statutory regulations and legal sanctions protecting the public interest against abuse. It is likely that every enterprise would be required to comply with universally applicable environmental, health, and safety restrictions. Following the lead of Sweden, community, regional, and national planning boards, on which workers would of course serve, would in all probability set comprehensive policy guidelines. "Enlarged and actual citizenship in a multiplicity of participatory units," Pateman points out, "could give [the workers] concrete experience of the complex of interrelationships between different social spheres, roles and capacities."[34] In the words of a French socialist, "It would be a mistake to limit [workplace democracy] to production units; it aims higher. Its principle involves the whole society. It is the globalization of worker democracy, from the firm all the way to the highest level of decisions and including the political parties, public bodies, social service institutions, etc."[35]

Second, we find it inconceivable that the working class could win its claim to workplace democracy without its being embodied into law and thus reflecting the support of a substantial majority of the electorate. In order to uphold their cause's legitimacy within a democratic political context, workers must persuade the broad array of participatory groups that now exist and the relatively disinterested political community that worker participation will enhance the well-being of society as a whole. Consequently, workers would be ill advised not to interpret "worker participation" as sharing industrial decision making with such other affected groups as consumers, environmentalists, and other community interests.

Excessive influence of corporations on public policy and government that now exists would not necessarily disappear with the coming of industrial democracy. If we assume the continuation of a market system, each firm would certainly have the freedom to make decisions in accordance with its own best interests, which would tend to skew governmental operations in their favor. However, with the democratization of the corporate sector, the decision-making arena within each firm would be considered public rather than private space. Within this public and democratic space, all major public interests would have a voice in decision making, including consumers and local and regional communities. Outside public representation of this kind would tend to broaden the perspective of workers within the firm. Moreover, regional and national economic planning, which establish guidelines for corporate investing, would not be incompatible with the democratization of corporations, irrespective of whether they were privately, cooperatively, or worker owned. Corporate veto power would still remain a political factor, even when the workplace was democratized, but the extent of its control over democratic governments would in all likelihood be substantially diminished.

Despite these safeguards, is there not a likelihood that workers in self-governing enterprises would jeopardize the interest and stability of their firms by exercising their newly won authority to distribute an excessive amount of their annual surpluses to wages or to other categories that directly benefit themselves? The empirical evidence on this question, although not extensive, does not support an affirmative answer. In recent years it has been more the rule than the exception for workers to make sacrifices in wages and other benefits in order to keep their firms afloat. Workers who own their firms have even greater incentives to sacrifice in order to save them and thus their jobs.[36] In noncrisis situations, when the stability of the firm is not threatened, workers remain cautious in reaching long-term decisions. The plywood cooperatives, for example, tend to put aside a greater portion of annual profits for reinvestment and unseen future contingencies than do conventional plywood firms.[37] Self-managed firms in Yugoslavia have also, with few exceptions, been prudent in allocating a relatively high share of annual surpluses for reinvestment.[38] The best example of this phenomenon is Mondragon, which comprises a network of eighty worker cooperatives in Spain. During the recession in 1981 workers made substantial sacrifices to keep their jobs, "digging into their own pockets to keep the balance sheets in shape."[39] To assure that workers' decisions in dividing annual surpluses are indeed prudent, Mondragon cooperatives are bound by a self-imposed rule that mandates that 15 to 20 percent is allocated to a reserve fund for the firm and another 10 to 15 percent is used for social and educational purposes.[40] These cases support Dahl's argument that "we can hardly deny that the losses incurred by workers from the decline of a firm are normally even greater than . . . investors suffer; for it is ordinarily much easier and less costly in human terms for a well-heeled investor to switch in and out of the securities market than for a worker to switch in and out of the job market. A moderately foresightful worker would therefore be as greatly concerned with long-run efficiencies as a rational investor or a rational manager, and perhaps more so."[41]

IX

In response to the charge that a democratic participatory system would enhance political fragmentation, we see no reason to suppose that fragmentation would be more pronounced in a democratic political culture favoring participation than it is today. Competition among firms and industries in a pluralist society is a fact of life, whether industry is governed hierarchically or democratically. Workers would probably follow the lead of their predecessors and form industrywide, national organizations as a way of regulating industry. However, worker organizations that led the fight for workplace democracy would logically play a decisive role as overseers of the new system and would vigilantly seek to maintain and advance the participatory and egalitarian gains within the larger industrial system. (For further discussion of the problem of political fragmentation, see Chapter 7.)

X

The moral distinctiveness of the representative system, according to Kateb, is that it "profoundly chastens" political authority. Together with millions of eastern Europeans, we agree that this is an invaluable function that a representative political system affords. But what criterion should be employed to determine whether governmental authority has been, in actuality, sufficiently chastened? To reply "free elections" only begs the question. For just what makes an election free? Is a mere contest enough when the competing candidates avoid substantive issues and only a bare majority bothers to vote? We find it disconcerting that a theorist of Kateb's stature shows little interest in exploring ways by which the representative system might be changed so that more people would be encouraged to join the politically active, thereby more effectively chastening political authority and making it more responsive to the needs of the disadvantaged strata of society.

We concur with Kateb's assessment of Rousseauian direct democracy. Its emphasis upon uniformity of interests and its disparagement of private space are hardly the appropriate preconditions for nurturing individual growth and free thought. However, for Kateb to argue that the Rousseauian concept of community is fundamentally flawed does not warrant the quantum leap, in the absence of supporting argument, to the conclusion that there is no "plausible vision of direct democracy [Kateb assiduously avoids the phrase 'participatory democracy'] that escapes Rousseau's constrictions of humanity."

Unlike Rousseau's community, which is unitary and all-embracing, our vision of a participatory society adumbrates a multiplicity of widely diverse democratic decision-making entities. There is no denying that any one group, especially because of its smallness, structured to accommodate face-to-face discussions can be oppressive and tacitly promote uniformity of ideas. An untenured faculty member of a small department, for example, may prudently take a back seat in collegial discussions and decision making. However, this problem can be resolved if, unlike the Rousseauian monolithic community, the faculty is organized democratically and comprises a plurality of decision-making units, consisting of councils, planning boards, unions, and the like. Democratic plurality provides relief from oppression and, equally importantly, affords an opportunity for individual members of society to find decision-making groups congenial to their interests and temperaments. To protect and encourage participation among those within low-status positions could lead to organization along status, skill, tenure, and salary lines. It is not uncommon in universities for undergraduates, graduate students, and untenured faculty to organize separately, and for each to send its own delegates to the appropriate decision-making bodies of the university.[42]

XI

In the formative stage of participatory theory its proponents overreacted to the liberal theorists' dominance. In striving to maximize citizen participation, they downgraded the importance, if not the legitimacy, of political leadership. Within a participatory society equality of power was intended to replace hierarchy. The leader's role, therefore, was limited to reflecting and implementing policy that was shaped in dialogue among equals, rather than in dictating policy from on high.

In the work of John Schaar a more vigorous concept of participatory leadership emerged. It conceives of a democratic relationship between leaders and followers in which "leaders and followers interact on levels of mutual, subjective comprehension and sharing of meaning. . . . [By] mutual identification, and coperformance, the leaders find themselves in the followers, and they find themselves in the leaders."[43] Grounded in this relationship, the primary function of leaders is to foster through their ideas and visions an educated, robust citizenry. Citizens in turn sustain their leader with their creative energies, essential to a vibrant public life. Thus, from a revised perspective of participatory democracy, close and regular dialogue and interaction between leaders and followers in the

choice and formulation of public issues and in the shaping
of public policies become the mark of democratic leadership.
Lao Tzu was not far from the mark when he said:

> A leader is best
> When people barely know that he exists,
> Not so good when people obey and acclaim him,
> Worst when they despise him.
> "Fail to honor people,
> They fail to honor you;"
> But of a good leader, who talks little,
> When his work is done, his aim fulfilled,
> They will all say, "We did this ourselves." [44]

The relationship of leader to led is predicated upon equality,
analogous, as Gramsci observed, with the relationship between
teacher and pupil, which "is active and reciprocal so that every
teacher is always a pupil and every pupil is a teacher." [45] He also
saw that in order for a political movement to achieve greater
equality in the distribution of power, the way the movement
itself is structured must already reflect the preeminence assigned to the value of equality. Therefore, democratic leadership must be seen as integral to the growth of collective rule
in all forms of communal life. As we pointed out before, one
of the most remarkable features of the civil rights movement
of the 1960s was the emergence of a large number of diverse,
committed, and articulate black leaders who seemingly ma-
terialized out of nowhere. The inference to be drawn from
this phenomenon, which is evident in other political movements—such as the labor movement of the late 1930s and,
more recently, the neighborhood, feminist, and environmental movements—is that grassroots leadership, fostered and
sustained by active followers, is, in embryonic form, a fundamental characteristic of a participatory democratic society.

Moreover, citizen involvement in public life not only nurtures grassroots leaders but can be expected to significantly improve the quality of national leadership. For, on all political levels, the quality of leadership is closely tied to the quality of followership. Thus, in sharp contrast to our present malaise, where citizen passivity and leaders without either the will or the capacity to lead interact to deepen our governmental paralysis, in a participatory society leaders are not likely to escape from confronting issues that have evolved through, within, and between countless publics (to use John Dewey's phrase) dispersed throughout the nation.

Although leadership and followership are clearly interdependent in our present political system, the failure of one cannot fairly be blamed on the failure of the other. We consequently disagree with Benjamin Barber, who contends "that a paucity of values that might sustain leadership" is not due to "a failure of leadership but a failure of followership, a failure of popular will from which leadership might draw strength." [46] And we disagree with the opposite position, which places the responsibility upon leadership. James MacGregor Burns holds that the so-called failure of followership can be overcome by the "transforming leader," who "taps the needs and raises the aspirations and helps shape the values—and hence mobilizes the potential—of followers." [47] Neither Barber nor Burns appears to consider that the failures of both leaders and followers reflect the disintegration of a nonparticipatory, elitist political system.

It seems strained to place the blame for the pallid character of American leadership, as Barber does, on the political passivity of the public, which fails to spur a dynamic leadership—when ordinary citizens lack the institutional means to determine their real interests. Conversely, one must be somewhat quixotic to depend, as Burns does, on the emergence of a "transforming leader"—an Abraham Lincoln or a Franklin Roosevelt—each time the polity is in desperate straits. Even if the transforming leader emerges in time to confront an

urgent and dramatic crisis—and that is a matter of chance—
the leader's success in mobilizing the people behind him or
her depends upon their state of mind. Mikhail Gorbachev's
struggle to remain in office illustrates the point. Prior to the attempted coup in 1991, the power resources at his disposal were
immense, rivaling Stalin's. But, given the emerging democracy
in the Soviet Union at that time, he lacked a crucial ingredient
of effective rule, namely, authority. As leader, he has been unable to acquire the crucial attitudes that undergird authority
in a democracy—the trust, confidence, and admiration of the
people.

Gorbachev's situation illustrates that gifted leadership not
only depends upon a transforming leader but also upon the
psychological capacity of followers to empower a leader and
thereby dramatize and enact the "interdependence of leadership and followership." We do not disparage the role of democratic leadership in the promoting and nurturing of citizen
participation. On the contrary, we strongly believe democratic
leadership to be strategically important in this regard. However, the significance of leadership as a democratic force is lost
when seen only as a catalyst to mobilize the people *within the
constraints of a ruler/ruled system*. This in effect is Burns's analysis when he contends that mobilization within the constraints
of the system promotes the substantive interests of the people.
The theory of democratic leadership should rather focus upon
citizens' liberation from rule by others and their transformation into a society determined by collective self-rule. The
potential of democratic leadership is most fully realized when
the commitments and energies of democratic leaders are directed in concert with their followers toward the elimination
of the institutional and psychological barriers that sustain and
reinforce the permanent separation between rulers and ruled.

To attempt to rebut this line of argument on the grounds
that a decline in the barriers between rulers and ruled would
lead to a "surge of democracy" and thus create an "overload"
of the political system is not tenable. This thesis, which Samuel

Huntington has made famously his own, is vulnerable on several counts. First, it is ahistorical. Increased policy polarization
was an outgrowth of the expanded political participation of
the 1960s, as Huntington claims, but the same phenomenon
also occurred during other eras of American history, such as
the New Deal. During the latter period increased participation and polarization led to a revitalization of democracy—
manifested, among other things, by a more responsive government—not to a "distrust and a sense of decreasing political
efficacy among individuals" as in the 1960s.[48] In the light of
this contradictory evidence, it could very well be true that it
was not the polarization in the 1960s that was the principal
cause of decreasing participation in the 1970s, as Huntington asserts, but rather that diminished citizen involvement
was a *reaction* to the unresponsiveness of government to the
people's needs. Second, Huntington takes great pains to show,
on the contrary, that government was indeed responsive to
the people's demands, otherwise one could not account for
the "Welfare Shift," which was primarily reflected in the dramatic rise in the welfare rolls. What he fails to consider is
the possibility, supported by considerable evidence,[49] that the
government was not responding to the needs of the ghetto
population, but to the threat of riots by the poor. Finally, the
overload theory takes the supply side as a given, ignoring the
government's option to tax. Huntington is right that the excess of expenditures over revenues was a major inflationary
source that plagued the United States in the early 1970s. But
since our tax rate at that time, as is true today, was relatively
low compared with other industrial nations, the so-called overload could have been rectified by increased taxes. If indeed
the source of the "democratic surge" was from below, it could
have mandated a progressive income tax designed to dampen
inflation and at the same time provide ample governmental
revenue for social needs. The deficiency was not in the capacity of the government to act, as Huntington argues, but
stemmed from an inadequacy in the intensity and breadth of

the "democratic surge." What was needed was more, not less, democracy.

Saddled by an all-time high federal deficit—caused by the Reagan administration's insatiable defense needs (hardly to be identified as the product of "a democratic surge"), the nation is once again burdened by governmental "overload." Ironically, it serves as an effective, although to some extent symbolic, restraint against adequate governmental aid to the poor. Consequently, Huntington's analysis of the causal relationship between popular participation and overload should be reversed: it is not that excessive participation creates overload; it is rather that overload effectively dampens popular participation. For since the federal deficit is thought to impair government's capacity to act, the incentive for lower-income groups to engage in political activity is curtailed. Again, the impasse can be broken only when it is publicly recognized that the fiscal limitations on government's capacity to act are self-imposed. Until this constraint is lifted by, for example, the enactment of a progressive income tax statute, overload will remain an effective instrument to sustain a niggardly governmental stance toward the social, economic, and environmental needs of society.

XII

It is clear from our defense of the theory of participatory democracy that the assumptions and principles underlying it and the theory of representative democracy are in sharp tension with one another. Nevertheless, it is equally clear that on a practical level each theory is dependent upon the other. Given the factor of size, in a large democratic society that requires the establishment and maintenance of representative institutions, we are emphasizing the importance of nurturing widespread political participation as an essential means of fostering a democratically responsible and responsive representative system of governance. A democratic participatory system committed to the promotion of self-development and the well-being of all of its citizens would aim to establish participatory institutions wherever practically feasible, and thus serve as a continuing democratic leaven on the representative system.

The Structural
Mobilization of Bias

3

I

It is not an exaggeration to say that the primary source of corporate power stems from the corporation's preferential role within liberal democratic power structures rather than from its own resources. Conversely, the relative powerlessness of ordinary citizens does not stem primarily from their lack of resources—their resources in numbers, after all, are potentially great—but from the political rules of the game that supply a powerful deterrent to the effective use of these resources. However, while existing political power structures in the United States constitute effective barriers to democratic change, they are not immutable. Although these power structures work to shape political outcomes, they, too, are vulnerable to transformation from within.

Preliminary to our discussion of the role of power structures in American politics, we first attempt to clarify the meaning and interrelationship of the concepts of power, participation, and power structure.

II

There is no noncontroversial definition of power. It is an essentially contestable concept, similar to other key political terms like "justice," "equality," "democracy," and "participation."[1] Definitions of key political concepts are unavoidably contestable since they are designed, consciously or unconsciously, to support particular political paradigms. The democratic liberal's (formally called pluralist's) definition of power is unacceptable to advocates of participatory democracy. This difference is understandable given the conflicting paradigms to which the two schools give their allegiance. Liberals seek to uncover, in any given polity, who rules: a unified elite or a plurality of elites. Their definition of power therefore focuses on power wielders—on who gets what, when, and how—rather than on those who are on the receiving end of power. In contrast to the liberals, participatory theorists focus primarily on those affected by power, on those who are left out of the decision-making process and on how they are left out and by whom. Participatory theorists are also concerned to explore the linkage between those who exercise power and those who are affected by it because they want to know what power mechanisms are responsible for adversely affecting subordinate groups. The definition of power advanced by these theorists, as we shall see, is therefore substantially broader than the liberals' definition.

Despite their conflicting conceptualizations of power, liberals and participationists agree that power is a relational, as opposed to a possessive, term, that such things as wealth, knowledge, and weapons, which can be possessed, are resources of power, but not power itself. They become an integral part of power only when power is exercised in relation to someone else.

There are three relational aspects to power. First, there must be a conflict of interest between two or more agents, since if the agents agree on a given course of action, power in an overt sense has not been exercised. Second, a power relationship requires that *B* bows, under threat of sanctions, to *A*'s demands. This attribute of power highlights one of its major advantages: as an instrument of intimidation and control it can be successfully exercised without depleting (in fact, it can even increase) the resources of its wielder. A mere conflict of interest, however, will not generate an exercise of power, if *A* cannot prevail upon *B* to comply with her demands. If B does not, a power relationship does not exist. Third, the existence of a power relation depends upon the value priorities of those on the receiving end of the power relationship. They are most likely to comply with *A*'s wishes when they believe that *A*'s threatened sanctions will deprive them of a value or values that they regard more highly than those protected by noncompliance. It is not an exaggeration to say, for example, that the United States lost the war against the North Vietnamese and the Viet Cong because American policy makers totally failed to grasp this point. They either were unaware of the value priorities of the enemy or failed to take those priorities seriously. If they had understood the values of the Vietnamese and the Viet Cong, the American high command would have realized that the killing of enemy troops would not in itself bring them to the peace table. Even death was an insufficient deprivation, outweighed, in the eyes of the Viet Cong, by a higher priority value—national independence—which they achieved only by not knuckling under to our death threats. In effect, our failure to comprehend the nature of power led to our inability to marshal power effectively.

As defined by Robert Dahl, a leading liberal who now embraces key tenets of participatory theory, power is exercised when *A* is successful in getting *B* "to do something he would not otherwise do."[2] Along the same lines, Nelson Polsby states, "One can conceive of power . . . as the capacity of one actor to do something affecting another actor, which changes the probable pattern of specified future events. This can be envisaged most easily in a decision-making situation."[3] Thus, in accordance with this conception of power, the central task for the researcher is to study decision making. For since it is assumed that (1) decisions reflect explicit and observable conflicts of interest, and (2) interests are policy preferences, it follows that actors whose interests prevail in decision making are relatively powerful.

The liberal conception of power seems to foreclose the possibility of a power elite at work in American politics and is supportive of the claim that political pluralism is alive and well in America. Among the numerous empirical studies conducted by liberals, we know of none acknowledging that the polity under investigation was ruled by a single elite. Instead, they conclude that key decisions are made by several, if not many, elites. This conclusion is due in large part to their focusing on decision makers and their ignoring those who are on the receiving end of power. Were this orientation reversed and theorizing and empirical investigations to center on the impact of key decisions on ordinary people, the findings might be quite different. For decisions made by a plurality of elites may appear, *when viewed from below,* to be the same as decisions made by a unified elite in one important respect: the decisions are all adverse to the interests of those who must obey. It is doubtful, for example, that urban ghetto dwellers discern any pluralism in various decisions that affect them which are issued by the health, welfare, housing, and school authorities. From the perspective of urban ghetto dwellers, it would appear that "pluralism" and class rule are entirely compatible, even somehow mutually supportive.[4]

By focusing on decision making to discover who "has" power, the liberals overlook a dimension of power that, as a rule, is even more encompassing and effective than the power that is exemplified in the making of decisions. It is an exercise of power that prevents dangerous issues from even gaining access to a relevant decision-making arena.[5] In effect, "nondecision" becomes an application of power, since it confines decision making to issues that do not threaten the interests of dominant groups. Defenders of the status quo may be engaged in the process of affecting nondecisions without being aware of it. Simply supporting established political processes—which may constitute a "mobilization of bias"—would tend to have this effect.[6] By failing to consider nondecisions in their studies of power, pluralists were unable, in other words, to assess with accuracy the degree of power exercised by decision makers.

By defining interest in terms of explicit policy preferences, the liberals reinforce the restrictive nature of their conception of power. For if power is expressed only as an *observable* conflict of interests and interest is reflected solely in *explicit* policy preferences, the study of power is justifiably confined to an examination of who prevails among those who express conflicting policy choices. In accordance with this line of argument, it follows that a political issue cannot exist unless and until an overt controversy surfaces within the political arena.[7]

From this narrow perspective, covert issues—that is, issues that are discussed and debated among ordinary people but that do not succeed in achieving an overt translation into the political arena—become nonissues that may safely be ignored by the researcher. However, by neglecting these issues, the researcher is insensitive to the possibility that power has been exercised from above in subtle ways to keep the issues submerged and thus out of the political arena. The analyst consequently is unable to determine whether the configuration of power in a particular community is pluralistic or elitist. This omission is especially disturbing to the participatory theorist, whose understanding of the phenomenon of nonparticipation would be substantially enhanced by studies that illuminate the impact of various forms of power on nonparticipants.

Another major deficiency in the liberal conception of power is its rejection of the common-sense notion that people might be mistaken concerning what constitutes their interests. That is, it fails to take into account the possibility that through processes of socialization and manipulation, people's interests can be shaped without their realizing it. Accordingly, power must be conceptualized in both its decision-making and nondecision-making aspects, visible and invisible forms. Formulated in this way, power is being exercised covertly when *B* conforms to the wishes of a power wielder of whose very existence *B* may be unaware. More specifically, it is covertly exercised over *B* when he is adversely affected by a nondecision and thus unaware of the suppressed issue, even when it shapes or determines his very wants.[8] To accommodate this broader and more indirect conception of power, we can describe power as follows: *A* exercises power over *B* when, in her own interest, she gets *B* to do something that is contrary to *B*'s interests.[9] Conceptualized in this way, it becomes apparent that power can be exercised even when there is no *overt* conflict between *A* and *B*. Furthermore, it can be exercised by *A* over *B* although *A* neither intends to affect *B*'s interest nor benefits from burdening *B*. *B* may be totally unaware that *A* is limiting *B*'s interests.[10]

In contemporary politics these characteristics of power are manifested in many plant closings. An employer closes his steel mill because it is not profitable to operate. In doing so, he not only adversely affects the interests of his workers and the people in the immediate community, but also the farmers who live one hundred miles away and are unaware that the steel mill has closed. Here, let us assume, there is no overt conflict between either the employer and the community or the employer and the farmers. The employer does not intend to exercise power over either group, nor does he benefit from their losses. Yet the adverse effect on both the community and the farmers is unmistakable; power has been exercised.

This conception of power, in sharp contrast to the liberals' notion, is oriented toward the major concerns of the participationists. Given their broad view of what constitutes power and their focus on those affected by it, this conception of power is a more effective investigative tool to measure to what extent power is exercised, how and by whom, to deflect ordinary men and women from engaging in meaningful political participation.[11]

This radical conception of power, however, presents us with an awkward problem, namely, what constitute B's real interests and who should decide what these interests are? If we do not know B's real interest, we are unable to determine in any given case whether power has been exercised against her. Resolving this question confronts us with a dilemma. We cannot accept, on the one hand, the preferences expressed by individuals concerning what constitutes their real interests, since their beliefs may sometimes be a product of manipulation. On the other hand, however, we are unable to subscribe to the view that experts are more qualified to judge the real interests of individuals than individuals themselves are. We are told by experts, for example, that smoking is contrary to our real interest. But this statement is true only if our values are such that our good health outweighs the satisfaction, derived from complying with the norms of one's group, that we believe can be furthered by smoking. Unfortunately, a "true" value preference—for example, good health over an immediate satisfaction—is not subject to final validation.

Given the validity of Mill's dictum—that in the last analysis individuals are the best judge of their own interests—one must ask what guides or standards there are, if any, for a person to decide what his real interests are. One such guide is provided by William Connolly's definition of real interest. He states: "Policy x is more in A's real interest than policy y if A, were he to experience the *results* of both x and y, would choose x as the result he would rather have for himself."[12] Connolly's definition is clearly a start toward providing a useful way to determine real interest. Unfortunately, however, it does not take into account the effect of various forms of power on choice.

It is not applicable, for example, in a situation where the preferred choice of *A* between policies *x* and *y* is made in order to avoid a threat of sanctions. Nor is it applicable—to cite the case of smoking again—when power has already been exercised in shaping individuals' wants and desires. In other words, to the extent that individuals' preconceptions are a function of a social system, it is unlikely that their "rational" choices reflect their real interests.[13]

On a purely theoretical level these dilemmas might defy resolution. Pragmatically considered, however, the dilemmas themselves should alert us to the connections that subsist between power and choice. The dilemmas underscore the need to assess which political structures, principles, and processes are best suited to create conditions that minimize power constraints and through participatory involvement foster people's understanding of their real interests.

III

In their well-known work *Participation in America*, Sidney Verba and Norman Nie formulate a liberal definition of participation, as "those present activities by private citizens that are more or less directly aimed at influencing the selection of governmental personnel, and the action they take."[14] What is most dramatically excluded by this definition is direct citizen involvement in decision making. The above definition is geared strictly to a representative system in which the overwhelming majority are assigned a limited participatory role in politics: that of periodically sharing in the selection of leaders and, for those in a position to do so, attempting from time to time to influence their actions. As we shall see in a later section of this chapter, this limited conception of participation has had a profound effect on shaping power relations within both the political realm and society as a whole.

From a participatory democratic perspective—in contrast

to the liberal representative conception—participation may be defined as action through which members of political structures, organizations, and groups effectively exercise power to influence policy outcomes.[15] In this definition power is used in two distinctive ways, as "power to" and "power over." "Power to" is equivalent to the ability to act effectively. Within a participatory context, it is the ability to express oneself intelligently in interacting with others to shape a common policy. Participatory theorists emphasize that power to participate effectively and democratically is an acquired trait that individuals gain from participation and, as a result of the participatory experience, develop more fully as individuals and citizens.[16] This argument not only illuminates the close linkage between power and participation but also the close relationship between power and participation, on the one hand, and freedom, on the other. This relationship is evident in the participatory process since the *power to* participate presupposes the freedom to exercise such power. However, owing to the narrow and limited participatory opportunities in the existing political system, meaningful participation is denied major strata of the population. This denial poses a key question (which will be grappled with later) that concerns the proponents of participatory democracy: How can power be effectively exercised *over* status quo defenders of the existing political system so as to construct new participatory structures—structures that would expand the freedom of ordinary people to exercise their *power to* participate? Once such structures have gained a foothold— in industry, for example—then the process could be reversed: the *power to* participate could become a valuable resource to generate greater *power over* the opponents of the expansion of participatory structures.

In our definition of participation, the phrase "members of political structures, institutions, and groups" is to be sharply distinguished from the traditional notion of "political." The political sphere, as distinguished from the civil or private one, is usually identified as that area which relates to government, thus excluding, for example, corporations as public organizations. Proponents of democratic participation have expanded this concept of the "political" to include all groups in society.[17] (This conception of the "political" is discussed in Chapter 7.) The clause "effectively exercise power" in our definition underscores that "power over" does not necessarily result from participation. Participation may occur without necessarily involving power when its outcomes are symbolic, that is, when outcomes do not impinge upon the distribution of power either within or outside the organization. Participation may also be repressive, as we will see, when workers' participation permits the authority and domination of management to increase. Here, indeed, participation involves power, but in a form that works against the participants' interests.

Ironically, participatory theory runs the risk of promoting symbolic and repressive participation. This tendency exists because the theory's twin objectives—of enhancing self-awareness and self-esteem, on the one hand, and communal self-rule, on the other—can be contradictory. The contradiction is manifested when the members of a group intent upon exercising their *power to* participate are unaware of how their participation handicaps their capacity to exercise *power over* those who control their lives. For example, workers who have been granted by management an increase in decision-making responsibility on the shop floor may be unaware that this action may legitimate increased managerial control over their lives. To correct this contradiction, participatory theory must distinguish between repressive and genuine participation, recognizing that the latter exists when self-awareness *and* communal self-rule are promoted at the same time. But in practice it is not easy to evaluate whether these goals are in tension with one another or are being advanced simultaneously.[18]

The meaning of "policy outcomes" in the definition is crucial to the participationists' position. Policy outcomes may be of two kinds: they may be produced in conformity with the general rules of the polity and without disturbing the political system, or they may effect change in political structures, transforming the rules of the game. In contrast to the liberal conception of political participation, which assumes that the rules of the game are given and focuses on the first category of outcomes, participationists emphasize the importance of the second category. They argue that the existing rules of the game now enforced in the American polity are basically class-biased and thus must be radically changed if democracy is to advance and to flourish.

IV

Essentially, power structures are composed of long-term, relatively persistent sets of values, doctrines, rituals, institutions, organizations, procedures, and processes ("rules of the game") that constrain and empower agents in the use of power. There are three major characteristics of power structures: The first is that power is wielded by human actors, not by structures. Power presupposes a certain degree of freedom for both A and B. It is exercised only if A and B are free to make choices: A to invoke power and B to comply or defy A's command. Structures, on the other hand, both empower and place limits on the range of options open to a power wielder. Bowles and Gintis evoke the analogy of chess to highlight the relationship between "structure" and "power." "The game of chess . . . is both an activity (playing chess), and structure (rules of chess). Unlike the games referred to in everyday language, however, we participate in most of the games that make up society not by choice but involuntarily." [19] A second feature of a power structure is that, unlike the rules of chess, the rules governing the exercise of power in society operate asymmetrically, benefiting certain players, who enjoy a preferred position, at the expense of others. [20] As Schattschneider put it in his famous dictum on the nature of a political organization: "All forms of political organization have a bias in favour of exploitation of some kinds of conflict and the suppression of others, because organization is the mobilization of bias. Some issues are organized into politics while others are organized out." [21] The third is that power structure, like power, should be seen primarily as a relational concept. The difference between the two is essentially that a structural relationship is broader and tends to be more permanent than a power relationship. In power relationships a wife may comply with the wishes of her husband to avoid his threatened sanctions. A structural perspective on the relationship would emphasize that the behavior of both husband and wife is more or less determined by the power structure in which they are embedded. The power structure of marriage is seen as the source of both the husband's power and the wife's compliance. However, as we will argue, this does not mean that in a particular instance either the husband or wife will necessarily conform to the stereotypical pattern of behavior prescribed by the marital power structure. That is, unlike the rules of chess, exercising power in the course of playing the game of politics broadly conceived may under certain conditions undermine and transform the rules. [22]

Classical Marxism would disagree with this assertion, which assumes that human agents have some autonomy to act outside the limits of a power structure and that when they act in accordance with their intention, they might actually change the structure. Adhering to a rigid determinist position, classical Marxism—in contrast to more humanist interpretations by most neo-Marxists—argues that agency is an illusory category, and thus it is held to be nothing short of absurd to say that human agency has the capacity to deflect the objective forces of history. The causal relationship is perceived as being the other way around: objective forces shape and direct human action. As Marx succinctly put it: "Men make their own history, but they do not do so as they please." For classical Marxists, the ultimate role of "historical agency," which the emerging proletarian class constitutes, is to carry out its revolutionary mission as it is developed and sharpened by the growing and irresistible tensions surrounding the productive forces of society.[23] Even the revolutionary class is thus shaped in large measure by objective forces and conditions.

A significant difficulty with this position is that the proletariat, especially in periods of economic crisis—when this class is expected to occupy center stage—does not always get the "correct" message from the ostensibly "objective forces." This point was dramatically etched upon Antonio Gramsci's mind when, in the late 1920s, he watched the Italian fascists, not the communists, exploit the economic crisis leading to their capture of the state. From that traumatic episode Gramsci recognized that rather than leading automatically to social revolution, economic and political crises create political space in which people have an opportunity to shape their own destiny. Realistically viewed, he believed that the ruling class is more strategically placed than is the working class to exploit social and economic instability for its own advantage. In Gramsci's words: "The crisis creates situations which are dangerous in the short run, since the various strata of the population are not all capable of orienting themselves equally swiftly, or of reorganizing with the same rhythm. The traditional ruling class, which has numerous trained cadres, changes men and programmes and, with greater speed than is achieved by the subordinate classes, reabsorbs the control that was slipping from its grasp. Perhaps it may make sacrifices, and expose itself to an uncertain future by demagogic promises; but it retains power, reinforces it for the time being, and uses it to crush its adversary."[24]

When class struggle takes place within the context of a democratic polity, Gramsci might seem overly pessimistic in his judgment that established elites have an overriding power advantage over working-class groups in periods of crisis. We will examine this point later on. Here we want to observe that Gramsci's argument limiting the scope of structural determinism in periods of crisis has been convincingly expanded upon by a contemporary Indian neo-Marxist to include normal periods as well. Sudipta Kaviraj points out that historical determinism (which we have called structural determinism) "never determines in a categorical fashion what is going to happen: it refers to what cannot happen."[25] This formulation might appear to be inconsistent, since excluding what cannot happen already delimits to some extent what can happen. But it is the force of the "to some extent" that is significant: structural determinism can describe only a range of what might happen, nothing specific or categorical. Thus Kaviraj concludes that "determination" must be seen as a *negative* concept. "It fixes ranges of possible choice or outcomes. We denote by determination not the event, but the space allowed to the event; not what must take place, but the margin within which it must occur."[26] Translated into our terminology, a power structure sets the range of options open to both the exercisers of and compliers with power. Within the ideological structure of capitalism, for example, employees who are evicted from a plant closed by the employer have certain options, but they are precluded by the "rules" from destroying or seizing the plant. Within an academic power structure, students likewise have a limited number of actions available to rectify their grievances. Rarely if ever can they get poor teachers dismissed or effect a decrease in tuition. Within the marriage power structure—even under today's more liberalized rules—the options open to a wife in a divorce are still quite limited; they almost never include receiving compensation for homemaking and childrearing, nor an equal share in her husband's future income. What is common to all these power structures is that the options of those who are on the receiving end of the power relationship are narrowly limited. However, as we have pointed out, structures in liberal democratic regimes can be breached and changed by the marshaling of power spurred by the democratic conviction of subordinates.

Structures can be divided into two categories: They are either institutional, such as corporations, government, and voluntary associations, or abstract, such as democracy, liberalism, constitutionalism, market, and class. The two structural types tend to reinforce one another. For example, the president of a large corporation is powerful owing to the range of options afforded him as its head. The corporate power structure in turn is sustained and nurtured by a liberal-oriented abstraction, namely, the sanctity of the private sector, which precludes the government from interfering with such crucial corporate decisions as investments.

The mystique of the corporate structure as private space, and therefore inviolable, constitutes an extension of the liberal doctrine, which envisages society as divided into two spheres: the civil or private, and the political or public. (See Chapter 7 for an extended discussion of this division.) Liberal theory attaches primacy to the civil sphere because it is here that all members of society, with their individual aims, interests, and ambitions, have free space to pursue happiness. To protect the pursuit of happiness, which is overwhelmingly identified with the right to acquire and own property, has become the principal function of the liberal state. This state function evokes the image of a necessary evil to be tolerated to the extent that it enables the embodiment and personification of the individual, the corporation, to pursue its private ends. As John Kenneth Galbraith puts it: "A great gulf is deemed to divide the state and the business firms. Only in the rarest instances does the accepted ideology approve the constraining action across this chasm."[27]

The liberal wall of separation between public and private persists in sustaining, despite the welfare state, corporate autonomy in crucial areas of decision making. Although corporate discretionary power has been restricted in a variety of areas, ranging from labor relations, safety, and health of employees to environmental protection, price fixing, foreign trade, and the like, the corporation remains almost completely autonomous in making decisions on key issues relating to the goals, use, magnitude, and allocation of investment.

The large-scale extensive corporate autonomy, stemming from its ideological location within the private sector safeguarded by liberal doctrine, has profoundly affected American democracy in three important ways. First, it provides the ideological backdrop for the legitimatization of corporate oligarchy. Since the corporation is located and deemed to be functioning within the private realm, its organizational structure and the processes it employs in reaching decisions are regarded as strictly its own concern. Democracy, as a conceptualization of how life is to be organized in public space, consequently has limited authority in relation to the corporate world. As long as the liberal ideological wall between public and private separates politics and economics, the potentially redistributive force of participatory democracy working to mitigate inequalities in power and privilege within the industrial sector is kept at bay. Liberal ideology works to preserve a depoliticized workplace. Within this captive, politically emasculated environment mapped by liberal ideology, it is not surprising that—as noted by both Adam Smith and John Stuart Mill—workers have failed to cultivate the speaking and organizational skills required to exercise effective citizenship.

The private nonparticipatory culture of the workplace functions to replicate itself psychologically in the mind-set and outlook of the workers. Like other people, workers tend to curtail their wants to accommodate the realities of their situation, and thus they refashion their wants in the light of what they "ought to want" as "free" agents. For example, the mere obtaining of a job confirms their sense of freedom, despite the minimal discretionary control that they retain over their working lives.

By acquiescing in their employers' control over them—rather
than challenging it as an invasion of their freedom and dignity
as rational human beings and as democratic citizens—they,
on the one hand, preserve the "integrity" of an alienated and
stunted self and, on the other, reaffirm and strengthen their
employers' hegemony over them.[28] Their bondage is ideologically rooted in the liberal conceptualization of private space.

Second, the chief source of government dependence on
business lies in the privatized corporate autonomy ratified by
liberal theory. The unequal power relationship between government and capital is not grounded primarily on capital's
ability to exercise power overtly, as ruling class or elite theories would have it, but is rather—less mysteriously and more
straightforwardly—a function of the capacity of individual
firms to decrease or reallocate capital investments.[29] For those
who manage government—regardless of their ideological persuasion—are dependent upon a reasonably high level of economic activity. A sharp downturn in the economy is typically
accompanied by a decline in popular support of the government and at the same time a decrease in tax revenues. To avoid
losing power, governments, rather than impose new taxes or
incur further debt, rely on businesses to maintain an adequate
level of investment. To that extent, corporations have a veto
power over government in that a loss of business confidence—
owing to governmental policies deemed by corporate elites
to be unfriendly to their interests—may well lead to a sharp
decline in corporate investments, thereby creating major problems for state managers.[30] When the French President François
Mitterrand in 1984 defied business interests by ordering an
increase in minimum wages and the nationalization of key
profitable industries, he was forced in a matter of months to
reverse his policy in the face of business's sharp decrease in
capital investments. Not that business, as an organized and
unified entity, engaged the government in open political war-
fare. Quite the contrary: in a "nonpolitical" and unorganized

manner, individual entrepreneurs, in separate responses to the government's policies and independent of the actions of other corporations, simply cut back on their investments.

The effect of this indirect, individualistic, seemingly non-political response of business to government reforms is to discourage government from taking action that will undermine "business confidence."[31] In fact, it creates a motivation for government to actively encourage business to invest. President Kennedy's income tax reduction for the higher brackets in 1961 is a case in point. As Lindblom pointed out, "In countless of ways governments . . . recognize that businessmen need to be encouraged to perform. . . . Although governments can forbid certain kinds of activity, they cannot command business to perform. They must induce rather than command."[32]

The liberal group orientation of politics tends to blind its advocates to the possibility that pluralistic politics and class domination can coexist. They are quick to point out, for example, that large corporations compete among themselves in pressure-group politics. This is indeed true. However, they fail to consider that when corporations are analyzed in terms of their collective impact on investments, they are revealed as wielding a political punch unrivaled by any other group. Liberals also fail to see that this major structural bias of the political system is founded upon liberal ideology that accords legitimacy to the private, autonomous conceptualization of corporate decision making.

Third, owing to the corporation's capacity for private and autonomous decision making, it has a substantial advantage in the strategic area of management-labor relations. Unlike most unions, the corporation can reach its decisions with comparative speed and effectiveness, and at minimum cost. For example, a business firm can exercise power over labor through layoffs, plant closings, and plant relocations by a decision of one or a few people in top management. For labor to mobilize its power, which in the last resort usually means to strike, the rank and file must be willing to take such action, through coordinated and collective action of its members. Furthermore, the members must commit themselves to active support of the union's demands for a possibly indefinite amount of time.[33] The difference in opportunity costs of participation in a struggle of this kind between corporate decision makers and union rank and file is immense.

Moreover, the source of corporate power tends to be stable—located in control of production or services—while the union's power must be generated anew, each time it engages in a strike. The corporation's power is mostly indirect and hidden; labor's is open, publicly assessable by its ability to sustain solidarity and discipline among its ranks during the course of a strike. As Offe concisely puts it, corporations "do not create power and definitions of interest as a result of an organized process of mobilization and internal discourse among members; they merely state power positions that are already established and interest definitions that are already decided on."[34]

Even when unions are strongly established, structural bias plays a central role in sustaining an asymmetrical power relationship in favor of business over labor. One of the main reasons for this is that government tends to favor the basic interest of capital in high profits over labor's interest in high wages, better working conditions, and shorter hours. High profits generally encourage business to increase investment outlays, while increased costs (to pay for higher wages, and the like) discourage such action. Further, increasing wages can fuel inflation. Thus both business and government, albeit for different reasons, are interested in keeping wages down.

Perhaps the clearest structural political bias in favor of business is the preferential position business enjoys in its relations with local governments. Cities, like private firms, compete with one another in an effort to prosper and to grow. Just as business firms try to maximize profits and minimize costs, city decision makers strive to maximize revenue and restrict nonprofitable services. This is another way of saying that business and the upper economic strata are prime contributors to the city's revenue and services, while low-income families are a drain on its revenue. Consequently, the city treats the two classes—business and low-income groups—very differently. Municipal governments pursue public policies in such dominant areas as taxes, zoning, education, and transportation that are attractive to business and the upper strata, policies that, at best, do not unduly harm the lower strata. A more humane approach is seen as deleterious to the city's interest since such strategy, promoting the welfare of lower-income groups, would have the effect of attracting low-income families from elsewhere into the city and thereby (owing to the need to increase taxes) lead business and upper-income residents to leave. To promote such a policy, a leading urban specialist argues, would be to invite bankruptcy.[35]

The structural bias in urban politics favorable to business, Clarence Stone argues, "affords a reasonable explanation for why public officials choose a course of action sought by the few but opposed by the many. The few are better positioned to bring off complex projects and achieve tangible goals." Put more generally, "business interests prevail not because a ruling-class network promotes pro-business proposals, but because governments are drawn by the nature of underlying economic and revenue-producing conditions to serve those interests."[36] In effect, it is argued, the interests of business and the upper classes are most compatible with the economic health, and thus the general well-being, of cities.

In most cities the electoral process enables grassroots and neighborhood organizations to put redistributive proposals on the public agenda. However, they are seldom passed, or, if passed, they are usually implemented in a token fashion. Again, it should be noted that the primary reason for this is not because of the intervention of business elites, but because the interests of the lower classes simply do not pay off either politically for individual officeholders or economically for the city as a whole.[37]

Notwithstanding the built-in power imbalance of urban politics, some urban scholars believe that mass involvement in politics should be kept to a minimum. Paul Peterson, a leading authority on urban politics, states this view forcefully. "To the extent that local politics weakens the capacity for mass pressures, it allows for due consideration of city economic interests. At times the interests of one or another notable may run contrary to the economic interests of the city as a whole, but it is the interests of the disadvantaged which consistently come into conflict with economically productive policies. By keeping mass involvement at the local level to a minimum, serious pressures for policies contrary to the economic interests of cities are avoided."[38] Peterson is not saying that he personally favors the interests of notables over those of the lower classes. He is arguing rather that within the context of the structural constraints that define city politics, the interests of the upper strata—in sharp contrast to the interests of other groups— are in accord with and promote the economic well-being of the city.

But this argument rests upon a highly debatable assumption: that the urban political structure is a given, to be accepted and not questioned. The concept of power is also taken as a given in this analysis; it operates within and in accordance with the rules of the structure, not as an instrument for transforming the structure. Thus, as an "objective" scholar, Peterson argues that the structure must be identified and acknowledged and the rules that govern it must be adhered to, in order to maximize the economic well-being of the city. In affirming the structure's immutability, he reinforces its legitimacy. He can ignore the class bias and undemocratic impact of the structure upon city politics as long as he continues to assume that the structure is indeed immutable. If, on the other hand, Peterson were to recognize that the structure could be transformed—

that power could be exercised to democratize the structure—
then the legitimacy problem resurfaces: should a class-bound
structure remain intact, or ought it be refashioned to make
it more responsive to democratic norms? Peterson avoids this
question.

Another class-biased structure, but one that appears neutral
and favorable to promoting pluralism, is the fragmentation
of the political system. In defense of the fragmented system
as being class neutral and fair, Nelson Polsby argues: "In
the decision-making of fragmented government—and American national, state, and local governments are nothing if not
fragmented—claims of small, intense minorities are usually
attended to. Hence it is not only inefficient but usually un-
necessary for entire classes to mobilize when the preferences
of class members are pressed and often satisfied in piecemeal
fashion. . . . The fragmentation of American governmental
decision-making and of American society makes class consciousness inefficient and, in most cases, makes the political
interests of members of the same class different."[39] Polsby is
right that, owing to the fragmented political system, "intense
minorities are usually attended to" and class conscious politics is inefficient. However, he fails to point out that empirical
evidence overwhelmingly shows that the "intense minorities"
most successful in gaining the attention of government are
corporations and that fragmented government affords penetration by powerful private interests at all levels of governmental decision making. It provides them with a strategic position
within government to oppose any broad-range proposal that
they may find hostile to their interests.[40] Fragmented government is not only vulnerable to being held captive by powerful
groups who assume vital positions of power within it but also
to being dominated by such groups from without. Lindblom
believes that the pivotal defect of the system is reflected by
"the ease with which opponents of any positive policy . . . can
obstruct it." And it is "the power of the corporate veto—facili-

tated largely by the autonomy of the business enterprise—
which is most effective and damaging to the system."[41]

In sum, powerful groups—including relatively small, well-
organized lobbies such as the Corps of Army Engineers, the
American Tobacco Association, and large corporations—enjoy
a preferred position in the American political system. Viewed
from another perspective, its fragmented structures, as Madison and his colleagues emphasized, serves admirably as a major
barrier against the people's organizing a politically effective
"majority faction."[42]

The most insidious—albeit most hotly disputed—structural
bias within the political system is the political participatory
structure. Those who view this structure as biased and those
who believe it is class neutral agree on two important, but
seemingly contradictory, findings: (1) The rights and principles that constitute the participatory structure—the rights
of free speech and association, the right to petition one's government, the right to be a candidate for public office, and
the principles of one person, one vote and majority rule, are,
when considered as formal legal and constitutional guarantees, universal, and apply to all citizens equally and are therefore class neutral; and (2) "No matter how class is measured,
the studies consistently (and convincingly) show that high-
class persons are more likely to participate in politics than
lower-class persons."[43] With regard to interest-group politics—which is an integral part of the participatory structure—
there is also general concurrence with Schattschneider's conclusion that the "upper-class bias of the pressure system shows
up everywhere."[44]

Those who hold that the participatory structure is class neutral explain the discrepancy between the official neutrality of
the participatory structure and the unequal way it operates
by arguing that the underclasses are politically disadvantaged
because of their unequal position in the socioeconomic system, and not because the participatory structure itself is class

biased.[45] Since failure of these classes to fully exploit their participatory rights is rooted in a highly unequal system of distribution of wealth and income, it is argued, the focus should be on the issue of economic inequality, not upon the adequacy of the participatory structure. The class-neutral participatory structure, it is claimed, stands ready to be used in the struggle for equality. This belief is expressed forcefully by Verba and Nie: "Participation, looked at generally, does not necessarily help one social group rather than another. . . . It [the system] could work so that lower-status citizens were more effective politically and used that political effectiveness to improve their social and economic circumstances. . . . Participation remains a powerful social force for increasing or decreasing inequality. It depends on who takes advantage of it."[46] In effect, Verba and Nie are saying that if only the powerless had the political will to mobilize their numerical strength, they could gain the world. The participatory framework is there for the benefit of all—lower-status citizens must only choose to use it.

The weakness of this argument consists in its failure to consider that the choice to remain a nonparticipant may itself be shaped by the nonparticipatory system, for the system is too often perceived by subordinate classes as a system with little meaning or use for them in their everyday lives. Verba and Nie fail to see, in other words, that the ongoing participatory structure in which electoral agendas are almost invariably geared to the interests and concerns of upper- and middle-class voters and are more or less irrelevant to the lower-income strata not only helps those who are better off but also legitimates and reinforces the silence of those who are worse off.

The electoral process is steadily deteriorating. When an increasing number of lower-strata citizens do not vote, otherwise left-of-center candidates are discouraged from raising redistributive issues, which would be attractive primarily to lower-income voters. By fostering nonparticipation among these voters, the participatory structure serves indirectly to restrict campaign issues to subjects that are nonthreatening to the interests of the upper and middle classes. As this downward cycle of declining participation continues—and campaign issues therefore become less and less relevant to lower-class interests—the participatory process takes on a life of its own, becoming an independent force fostering nonparticipation. This regressive pattern has the dangerous effect, among others, of depriving the entire citizenry of exposure to and consideration of an important range of issues.

A major contributor to the class bias of the participatory structure is the significantly greater cost of participation to lower-class players than to upper-class players. As John Harsanyi puts it, "If some actors encounter less resistance than others, they must expend fewer resources to achieve their goals—in short, their opportunity costs are lower."[47] The opportunity costs, for example, for David Rockefeller are minimal when he can get what he wants by a phone call to a high political official. For him, political participation undoubtedly pays off and, moreover, requires little effort. In sharp contrast is the case of a lower-stratum neighborhood group that spent countless hours and considerable energy in its effort to pressure city officials to install a traffic light at a dangerous intersection in their neighborhood. Yet despite the reasonableness of their request and their vigorous participation over a period of time in an attempt to pressure local officials, the local officials remained unmoved. It was especially demoralizing that during the course of their struggles, in which their opportunity costs were excessively high and their returns zero, the city granted, with minimum pressure, a similar request by a middle-class neighborhood.[48]

Clearly, class is often a decisive factor in the participatory game: the lower the class, the greater resistance by public officials and the greater the cost to participate. Thus to compete equally in the participatory game, lower-strata citizens must be able to marshal greater power than their upper-class competitors. Worse still, in order even to get into the game, they must be willing and able to pay a comparatively high price. "Affluent, well-dressed business people or professionals," Jack Nagel writes, "can readily gain access to high officials who are likely to resemble and agree with them. Less polished laborers or clerks will find themselves cooling their heels before minor functionaries and flak-catchers. In short, people of higher status more often find that participation pays off. The process is easier and less threatening for them, and the results are typically more to their liking."[49] Besides the material benefits gained from participation, members of the upper and middle classes acquire through their participatory experience a greater sense of political efficacy and a better understanding of their real interests, which are discovered and affirmed through participation.

V

As we have argued before, a sustained working-class struggle to achieve workplace democracy is the most effective strategy to promote the realignment of the party system along class lines, to activate working-class people politically, and, in effect, to significantly dismantle the current mobilization of bias. However, at the outset, given the effectiveness of the mobilization of bias to prevent or restrain sustained mass political participation, our strategy is confronted by a dilemma that has haunted these pages: If working-class struggle to achieve workplace democracy is to be sustained over a period of time, there must be basic changes in the rules of the game; otherwise we are on a treadmill, with all efforts to realize this goal deflected in advance by class-biased rules. However, if the rules of the game are to be changed, vigorous and widespread political participation by workers and their allies is necessary. A resolution of this dilemma is examined in Chapter 9.

Workplace Democracy
in Europe

4

Worker participation in the decision-making processes of the workplace is firmly established in most capitalist and socialist industrial societies. Support for worker-participation programs—ranging from codetermination, collective bargaining, shop steward committees, workers' councils to a combination of these—has covered the political spectrum, from the political right to the militant left, from corporate to union leaders, and from intellectuals to heads of state. And, as one might expect, the concept of worker participation has hovered between two poles: from work democratization, conceived as a means to democratically reconstruct the economic order, to work humanization, designed to increase job satisfaction and productivity without disturbing the distribution of power between management and workers.[1]

From a historical perspective, the spontaneous organization of workers, peasants, and other ordinary citizens in periods of unrest has often had a revolutionary potential. As Hannah Arendt emphasized, a significant commonality shared by the American, French, and Russian revolutions was the emergence of people's councils as a spur and guide to revolutionary "action and order."[2] Workers occupied factories and organized worker councils or soviets in Russia in 1905 and 1917. Such councils also sprang into being in the Paris Commune in 1871; Poland in 1905; Germany, Hungary, Italy, and Ireland in 1919; Spain in 1936; Poland and Hungary in 1956; France and Czechoslovakia in 1968; Italy in 1969; Portugal in 1975; and once again in Poland with the rise of Solidarity in 1981. Even in the United States workers' seizure of factories during the New Deal period sent a tremor through the upper classes. The radical democratic thrust in each of these cases can best be explained by the fact that workers spontaneously took action to assure themselves a public voice. In sharp contrast to some existing worker-participation programs, the militant worker councils of the past emerged without exception from below.

Despite the high hopes of socialist theorists such as Antonio Gramsci[3] and Andre Gorz[4] in the revolutionary potential of these councils, most of them lived momentarily and died a natural death, while others were coopted by "friendly" unions or political parties.

In this chapter we briefly describe ongoing worker-participation programs that have developed in the postwar period in key western European countries. The discussion focuses on three questions: Have any of these programs actually been able to reorder the distribution of power in the industrial sector and within society at large? Has democracy been revitalized by labor's struggle to democratize the workplace? And, to be answered in a later chapter: what are the lessons for America in the European experience?

I.   Germany

Since the spontaneous rise of the "republic of works councils" (usually misidentified as "Soviet republics") during the upheavals of 1918–19, the German labor movement saw the establishment of codetermination and workers' councils as an essential step toward building a democratic society.[5] This idea received a new impetus after World War II with the founding of the unions confederation (DGB—the Deutsche Gewerkschaftsbund) in October 1949. The confederation declared that "only through the complete democratization of economic life could capitalism conform to a more equitable and more socially oriented society. . . . The installation of co-determination at all levels of society, from shopfloor, firm and industrial levels, through chambers of commerce and industry, up to public institutions . . . would give macroeconomic direction to the economy."[6]

A major victory for the unions occurred in 1951 with the enactment of an extensive codetermination law for the coal and steel industries, which established the kind of equality of voice in decision making for the two major industries that the DGB sought to extend throughout German society as a whole. The law provided for parity between capital and labor on boards of directors, and it authorized union nomination of a labor director—responsible for personnel relations, workplace safety, employee grievances, and so forth—on the day-to-day management board of each firm. Finally, it provided for a neutral member of the board of directors—appointed by both labor and capital—to cast, when necessary, the tie-breaking vote on the board.[7]

It was not until the mid-1970s that the trade unions, with the aid of the Social Democratic party, which was then in power, pushed through legislation that provided equal labor-management representation on the boards of all corporations employing more than 2,000 workers. The passage of the law constituted a significant setback for the trade unions since they were unable to gain full-parity codetermination. A key provision of the statute provides that the chairman of the board, who cannot be elected against the will of representatives of capital, has the decisive vote in deadlocks.[8] Thus capital sustained its control of industry. Despite their victory on the crucial issue of control, industrial leaders challenged the constitutionality of the codetermination law on the ground that it deprived capital of its right of property. In 1979 the Federal Constitutional Court held that since the law did not empower labor with full parity, it did not threaten the legal prerogatives of employers.[9]

Even though the law specified that only three of the ten labor representatives to corporate boards must be nominated by trade unions, in practice more than 80 percent are union delegates. With some justification, unions defend their dominant role in worker delegations on the boards on the ground that in the absence of union power, worker representatives on the boards would be stripped of influence. Undeniably, the workers' voice on the boards would carry less impact without outside organized workers' support. However, the present system of labor representation has led to a loss of communication between union leadership and the rank and file and a loss of interest on internal policy issues among the latter.[10] It is generally agreed among observers of German labor relations that under union tutelage the interests of union leadership and bureaucracy usually prevail over the needs of ordinary workers. In creating elite positions for trade unions, codetermination has fostered oligarchical tendencies within the union movement.[11]

It has also been found that union leaders have both aggrandized power to themselves and enriched themselves monetarily by occupying positions as board members in several enterprises.[12] In his thorough and perceptive study of the German labor movement, Alfred Diamant concluded that the achievements of codetermination "so far are more nearly system-maintaining then system-transforming in character. This has been so . . . primarily because the labor movement—at least since 1949—has moved almost entirely within a moderate, evolutionary ambience. . . . [Even] if full parity co-determination had been achieved it would not have been the occasion for radical transformation of the society and economy."[13] A German employer representative at an international confederence on worker participation remarked that it seemed to him "that after almost twenty-five years of codetermination in Germany, the employers seemed more satisfied with it than the unions."[14] The fundamentally conservative nature of codetermination is also attested to by a declaration issued by the German Trade Union Federation: "It is by no means the intention of co-determination to destroy the authority of management. . . . Nor is it intended that workers, acting through their delegates, should take over management. Codetermination also presupposes a system of free enterprise based on the principle of a free market economy."[15]

From the history of the German trade union movement in the postwar period it would appear that unions made the fundamental mistake of pushing for the enactment of a legalized structure of codetermination without paying sufficient attention to building a power base. "The unions seemed to think," Christopher Allen writes, "that if the law were only passed, then they would have more influence and control at the workplace. What the unions apparently did not fully realize was that effective influence and control depended not on the passage of a law but on the active mobilization and participation of their membership."[16]

Because of the union leadership's emphasis upon legislative and legal battles to obtain equal representation with capital on company boards, it is not surprising that German work councils, which are prescribed by law for all enterprises with more than five workers, tend to restrict rather than develop workers' participatory rights. Although elections are open to all employees, in practice 90 percent of the seats are filled by trade-union delegates. The councils have an equal voice with management on a wide range of matters, including job evaluation, working hours and overtime, social and welfare provisions in case of mass layoffs, training and accident prevention, and worker conduct on the shop floor. Furthermore, the council must be informed on all major policy areas involving technological changes, production programs, and the financial condition of the firm.[17] On the other side of the ledger, work councils are prohibited from sponsoring or organizing strikes and are required by law to promote a harmonious relationship between management and workers.

However, in practice, owing to union domination of the councils and the remoteness of council members from the rank and file on the shop floor, tensions have developed in some companies between the union bureaucracy and the workers. For example, the leader of an insurgent group in one of the larger steel plants in the country complained that "the established workers' council has too often given in to the company's logic. Workers' councils in big companies often seem to separate themselves from the worker and become managers. . . . In many plants the only thing that is missing is a spark for the fuse."[18] More than a few cases have been reported in which militant candidates standing for a council seat have successfully challenged union council members who had been in their positions for years.[19] These examples suggest that German work councils should not be written off completely as integrative structures in the workplace.

II. Sweden

The Swedish labor movement is extremely strong, in terms of its organizational penetration as well as in its political unity and ideological commitment. Sweden has the highest unionization rate of any western industrial society: 75 percent of the total labor force is organized. This large overall figure is attributable to the fact that more than 70 percent of white-collar workers are unionized. The power of the Swedish trade-union movement is considerably enhanced by its being highly centralized and owing to the close tie of its largest union (the Confederation of Swedish Trade Unions, or LO) with the Social Democratic party. Moreover, since nearly one out of every two Swedes is a trade-union member, center and liberal parties tend to follow the lead of the Social Democratic party on issues related to "Democracy in the Workplace."[20]

Because of the high degree of industrial concentration in the country, Swedish firms have been able to build a strong and centralized employers' confederation. Its power, which more or less balances that of labor, is reflected in its close and active involvement in the formulation and implementation of public policy. In 1984, for example, the Swedish Employers' Association had representatives on more than 200 central public agencies, councils, and boards. It was also represented on key ad hoc parliamentary committees and presented its position on proposals made by 132 parliamentary and other official committees on a wide range of issues.[21] Capital's and labor's both being institutions of countervailing power has resulted in a high level of institutionalization of labor relations in Sweden. Adhering more or less to corporatist theory, labor in effect renounced the strike weapon and has kept money wages and grassroots militancy down in return for capital's acceptance of the redistributive policies of the welfare state.[22] Both capital and labor benefited by the shift in labor relations in the postwar period from the industrial to the political arena. Labor gained, since the level of employment, which is crucial to the welfare of workers, can be controlled most effectively by fiscal and monetary measures, and thereby labor is at least partially freed from control by capital. Capital gained by governmental influence in sustaining stable labor relations and enforcing a noninflationary wage policy. It also valued the Social Democratic government's policy of granting large and efficient firms favorable terms for capital accumulation and expansion.[23]

However, by the mid-1960s, it became evident to both sides that the politically oriented, centralized bargaining system was unable to deal with issues on the enterprise level. The high and unprecedented proportions of rank-and-file absenteeism and turnover during this period spurred management to adopt major innovations in work structures.[24] The widely publicized Volvo experiments in Sweden involving direct worker participation in decision making on the shop floor were initially a great success. To a considerable extent, they achieved their aims of humanizing work and improving the quality of factory life. These gains were reflected in increased productivity and higher profits. However, the optimistic appraisals of these experiments were superficial to the extent that Volvo management refused to extend worker participation beyond the shop floor. Furthermore, it became evident that, with the exception of a small group of companies, industry was reluctant to adopt these experiments.[25]

In response to a rash of wildcat strikes in the early 1970s —largely protesting union bureaucratization—the Swedish unions abandoned their former position against codetermination and resolved to extend union participation to all levels in the workplace. Owing largely to labor's new militant stand, a series of codetermination acts were passed, culminating in the Democracy at Work Act of 1976. This law applies to large and small firms alike and requires management to engage in collective bargaining on all issues relating to the work environment and "other aspects of management."[26] If agreement is not reached in collective bargaining, labor has the option to strike. In the case of a dispute on the meaning of any clause of the agreement, the local labor union's interpretation of it is final. Another section of the law accords unions the right to select two representatives on the boards of most private firms. Unlike the German unions, the Swedish unions are not interested in equal representation, since they view union representation on boards as an important means to acquire information to be used to strengthen their position in future collective-bargaining sessions.[27] Under the provision of the law

that mandates training in economics and business administration for employee board members, unions have instituted
intensive training programs for their board representatives.[28]
Another act, which amends a previous safety law, provides
that the safety steward in each firm rather than management
or a government inspector has the right and responsibility
initially to halt any work that he or she considers to be posing a
serious danger. Furthermore, in any subsequent negotiations
on the issue, the burden of proof is on the employer, not on
the union steward.[29]

The most militant of the unions' proposals, commonly called
the Meidner plan, was introduced in 1976, but because of its
radical nature it did not become law until 1983, and then in a
highly modified form. Essentially the proposal called for the
establishment of a wage-earner fund, which would be financed
by a 20 percent tax on company profits and administered and
controlled by the unions. The proceeds of the fund would be
available to the unions to buy shares in profitable companies,
and in turn these shares would be collectively owned by the
employees. It was estimated that trade unions would become
majority stockholders in profitable companies within twenty to
thirty years.[30] The primary purpose of the plan was to reduce
inequality of income and power between capital and labor and
by so doing to increase labor's influence over the economy. At
the same time it was designed to enforce the principle of "solidaristic wage policy" that workers' incomes should not depend
on the profitability of the firm in which they are employed.[31]
In effect, its intention was to redistribute wealth from capital
to workers without being inflationary—workers would receive
increased power rather than increased money wages—without
either disrupting the solidaristic wage policy or diminishing
savings for capital investment. The innovativeness of the plan is
also marked by its aim to achieve increased democratic control
of industry without confronting the pitfalls of nationalization.

The public introduction of the Meidner plan in 1975, according to one report, "hit the Swedish political arena like a bomb. People became even more agitated when LO formally accepted Meidner's proposal at the 1976 Congress."[32] The plan was sharply attacked, especially by the business community. It discerned in the concept of collective ownership by workers a frontal assault against the principle of private property.[33] In addition, a key issue for business was its augmentation of union power at the expense of firms and how that power might impinge upon the implementation of national economic policy to the detriment of the political process conceived as a whole.[34]

Deeming the issue too hot to handle, the Social Democratic party resorted to the well-known delaying tactic of establishing an investigatory commission to study the matter further. It was not until 1983 that the Meidner plan was embodied in law, although as Rudolf Meidner commented, it was transformed into "a faint shadow of the original idea."[35] The fund is financed from a 20 percent tax on the profits of the larger firms in Sweden and from an additional 0.2 percent payroll tax. It is administered by five regional government-appointed boards (of which a majority are union representatives). To ensure that the fund would not be "confiscatory," the law provided that no board could own more than 8 percent of the shares of any given firm. Furthermore, the regional boards are barred from buying shares after 1990. By that time the funds will own no more than 10 percent of publicly held shares of Swedish corporations.[36]

The impact of the law has been largely symbolic. It has served psychologically to restrain wage increases, and it has, albeit marginally, diverted profits away from dividends and wage drift and toward potential job-producing investment. By the 1988 elections, the wage-earner fund became more or less a nonissue. According to a poll conducted prior to the elections, as many as thirty-nine of the top one hundred executives surveyed believed the Social Democratic party to be better for business than the opposition.[37]

It would appear that the cause of democratic worker participation in Sweden, except at the shop level, has been coopted by unions in their move to gain power. Instead of being confronted by the arbitrary rule of management, as in the past, Swedish workers now face a growing bureaucratically intertwined management-union cabal. It can be argued, however, that even under these circumstances, the potential for radical democratic change has nonetheless been advanced. This argument is based upon the plausible assumption that union leaders are more vulnerable than management to rank-and-file protest. Workers have successfully rebelled against the rigidity and unresponsiveness of union bureaucracies in the past and will undoubtedly do so in the future. But will this continue to be a never-ending cycle, with workers gaining substantive demands by pressuring the union, yet remaining unable to achieve greater direct control of their own work lives beyond the shop level? It is unlikely that the cycle will be broken unless, as we will argue later, the workers' rebellion is fueled by a clear vision of democratic participation and a strategy focused on wresting power from established elites, including labor leaders.

Although there are important differences in form between Germany's codetermination schemes and the Swedish system of collective bargaining, the outcomes of the two systems appear strikingly similar. Both systems have transformed the balance of power within the firm in favor of unions but have nevertheless preserved "the fundamentally capitalist nature of management."[38] In neither system have the workers themselves—as opposed to their representatives—gained a meaningful voice in determining the policies of the enterprise. Almost invariably there has been an intermediary—the union representative—and this circumstance has tended to maintain the traditional distance between ruler and ruled. However, the union elites' lack of attention to and concern for the development of participatory rights for rank-and-file workers can lead, as it has in the past, to effective rebellion from below. It is this democratic catalyst, as it impacts upon the strong Swedish trade-union movement, that is the key to the future development of industrial democracy in Sweden.

III.   France

The French labor movement is among the weakest in western Europe, in organizational penetration as well as ideological unity. Only 15 percent of the total labor force is organized, and there are three competing central union organizations with different political affiliations.[39]

The weakness of the French labor movement is reflected in its disappointing record, compared with other European labor movements, in securing participatory rights for its workers. When a socialist government was in office in 1981–86, it could take credit for the passage in 1982 of several laws designed to increase workers' freedom and rights in the workplace. At best, these were modest advances. The most important of these laws extended the powers of works committees that were created in 1945 as the prime framework for institutional participation. According to law, "The purpose of a works committee shall be to ensure that the employees can collectively express their views on the management and economic and financial policies of the undertaking, the organization of work and production techniques and thereby enable permanent account to be taken of their positions as decisions are reached."[40]

The works committee, which is elected by the staff as a whole, requires periodic open meetings between workers and management to discuss any issues that either side wishes to raise. Other than its right to participate in joint consultation on major issues in the firm, the decision-making power of the works committee is limited to health, safety, and working conditions on the shop floor.[41]

Employers and their professional associations initially opposed the passage of the so-called worker reform laws. But many employers rapidly had a change of heart when they saw that "right of expression" sessions were an effective way of promoting industrial peace and labor-management cooperation. For some employers, closer relationship with their workers became an effective tool to undermine the authority of unions on the shop floor and to gain workers' support for increasing productivity.[42] Other employers, who were not pressured by the unions, simply ignored the law requiring the establishment of works committees.

The half-hearted effort of French unions to establish another way of achieving meaningful participatory structures in the workplace was in sharp contrast to the spontaneous and massive uprising of workers and students in May 1968 in their demand for *autogestion* (economic democracy). It was conceivably the largest strike since the rise of capitalism. For both workers and students, *autogestion* was seen as a rebellion against the statist concept of revolution, which dominated French leftist discourse at that time.[43] It was "a vision of another way, a decentralized, classless, society composed of equal associations of self-governing men and women."[44] Although the French socialists recognized the need for political action, they were adamant in their belief that socialism would be advanced through struggle in the workplace and in the local communities, rather than from either maneuvers of parties and leaders or election results.

Autogestion was also thought of by French socialists as a means of recapturing the social man, which, according to Michel Rocard, had been destroyed "by dividing and isolating man into specific producer, consumer, and citizen roles. It is these divisions between civil society and political society, between concrete man and abstract citizen, that we must end. . . .

Autogestion is the means."[45] The democratic, decentralized, communal notion symbolized by *autogestion* had enormous popular appeal and at the time it was surprisingly successful in generating militant democratic activity in both private firms and the public bureaucracy.[46]

Autogestion also had a contagious effect upon all of the parties of the left who, at least rhetorically, embraced it. However, by the early 1980s it had disappeared from French politics as rapidly as it had risen in the 1970s. As George Ross put it: "Autogestion was like a bee that had flown noisily about the French political left after May–June 1968 until, after stinging everyone in sight, it died."[47]

Its demise can be attributed to at least three causes: First, as it grew in popularity, it became deradicalized, highlighting its antistatist and prodecentralization connotations and downplaying its connection with workers' control. Second, with the growth of middle-class interest in feminism, antinuclear power, and the environment, the problem of democratizing the workplace no longer commanded widespread public attention. Finally, and probably most importantly, confronted by the economic difficulties of the 1980s, François Mitterrand and his Socialist party colleagues underscored the need to nationalize a sufficient number of large firms as a means of managing the economy effectively, and thus, in Mitterrand's words, to control "the instrument for breaking the system of exploitation of man by man."[48] *Autogestion* was incorporated into the Nationalization Act of 1982—it mandated that the employees of each nationalized firm are entitled to elect one-third of its board of directors—but it was not taken seriously. Traditional management structure, for all practical purposes, was basically undisturbed in the nationalized firms. Disappointingly, the Mitterrand government did nothing to democratize these firms by delegating meaningful authority to worker councils situated at the plant or workplace sites. Thus the French socialists, who controlled the presidency and the National Assembly, turned their backs on a unique opportunity in modern history to further the cause of economic democracy.

Ironically, Mitterrand's timidity in not democratizing power in the nationalized firms may have led to the subversion of his nationalization strategy. Rather than adopt policy with the aim of securing democratic control of industry—which was the overriding purpose of nationalization—the new state managers of the nationalized firms "operated in all respects as private corporations facing competitive markets. . . . What was conceived initially as an instrument for attacking capitalist economic power became, under the Left, a device for reinforcing that power."[49] Mitterrand made the common mistake of assuming that the key to power is form and process rather than the cultivation of actors who have the power to manipulate form and process for their own purposes.

IV.   Italy

The spectacular rise of worker councils in Italy during the 1960s was fueled by oppressive working conditions, especially in the larger factories such as Alfa Romeo and Fiat, and by the social crisis of 1969. That crisis was triggered by the response of Fiat's management to a wildcat strike in one of the company's departments: engaging in overkill, management simply locked out the workers in Fiat's Turin factories. A wave of public sympathy was followed by widespread occupation of factories and schools. Martin Slater writes:

> The 1969 strikes were remarkable for the vigor with which they were fought. More remarkable still, the high level of activity did not collapse immediately in subsequent years as it had tended to do in other Western European countries. Sustaining this level of activity were new structures of workers' participation. These structures, consisting of shop-floor and factory assemblies, elected workplace delegates, and factory councils,

allowed much stronger expression of working-class interests. They also permitted a considerable broadening of the scope of topics raised in negotiations with public and private employers. Workers on the shop floor not only controlled the content of their grievances, but also, through their elected delegates, they fully controlled the negotiating process.[50]

The "hot autumn" of 1969 was soon cooled by the communists. Wresting control from the grassroots leadership of the newly formed councils and replacing them with union delegates, they helped "stabilize" the situation. The integration of the councils within the union movement was completed by the consolidation of the councils into larger organs, and the creation of higher-level coordinating bodies. This network of organizations has functioned as a valuable source of power for the communist unions in their negotiations with management. As Garson aptly puts it, this structural arrangement permitted the union's leadership to function effectively "without much possibility of rank-and-file intervention."[51] To extend union control to smaller firms, the Italian government passed (with the support of the Socialist party and the left wing of the Christian Democrats) legislation authorizing the existence of unions in all firms with more than fifteen employees.

The significantly increased union power in Italy has sharply encroached upon management prerogatives. Although management bitterly resisted each new penetration, Italian industrialists recognize, as do their counterparts in other European countries, that collective bargaining is not a fundamental threat to the stability of capital. This recognition was evident, for example, at the 1975 management seminar, sponsored by the OECD (Organization for Economic Cooperation and Development), on workers' participation. Commenting favorably on the state of collective bargaining, the consensus was that "in Italy collective bargaining at several organizational levels has become the main instrument of workers' participation, suggesting that collective bargaining can also become the main

tool of workers' participation in countries with a strong polar-
ized system."[52] In a more general vein, it was argued that,
in the interest of broadening worker participation, management should "make the trade union an important partner
within the enterprise and to have as regular and as exhaustive
negotiation as possible; and to extend the field of bargaining to a larger number of questions."[53] Within a climate of
labor unrest, the spiral of rank-and-file influence of unions
and the unions' influence in turn on management and left-
wing parties—a spiral that can be observed in most European
countries—is especially manifest in Italy. The spontaneous formation of worker councils in 1969 provoked a dramatic radicalization of trade unions—a reaction necessary for gaining
control of the councils. The unions' militant transformation
forced, on the one hand, management's adoption of a progressive worker-participation policy (as a cooptative strategy), and
on the other, the adoption by the Christian Democrats of a
conciliatory policy toward the Communist party, a strategy designed to prod the Communist party to continue to restrain the
trade unions.[54] Hence, we observe the formation of a reactive
sequence: Workers' spontaneity produces trade-union radicalization, which yields management proparticipation policies
and government appeasement of the Communist party. Then,
however, the combined influence of a more liberal management and a more conservative Communist party restrains
unions and, in turn, the rank and file. After a time worker
unrest builds up again and the spiral and reactive sequence
begin anew. (See Figure 1.)

The close collaboration of top union leaders with the
national government during the late 1970s and early 1980s
exacerbated existing tensions between the unions and the shop
steward committees. It reaffirmed the latter's determination
to maintain control of the shop floor, free from undue influence from union officials and management alike. Committee
members tended to believe that they knew more about factory-
centered problems and their solutions than union leaders

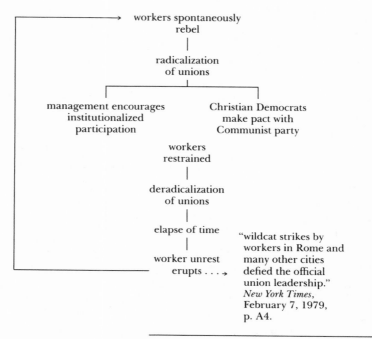

Figure 1: The Italian Cyclical
Participatory Pattern

coming from their headquarters in Rome.[55] This tension has
contributed to the formation of a bifurcated structure of labor
representation in Italy. On the one hand, there is the official
centralized union structure situated outside the workplace,
composed of three confederations, each consisting of a number of industrial unions that negotiate the national agreement.
Parallel to this, one finds the shop steward committees centered in the workplace itself, which are elected by all workers
regardless of their union affiliation, and which have acquired
the right to enter into agreements at the company, shop, or
office level.[56]

Although the power of Italian trade unions has declined

considerably since the early 1980s, owing largely to the shift in employment from large-scale industry to the tertiary sector and to small enterprises and to the widespread adoption of labor-saving technology, the degree of worker control of workplaces in Italy rivals that of analogous workplaces in Britain and Sweden.[57] However, as in Britain and Sweden, management authority in Italian firms is not challenged in such areas as investment decisions, industrial policy making, and strategic innovations.[58]

V.   Britain

The central characteristic of worker participation in postwar Britain was its lack of institutional and legislative support. This stemmed partly from the strong voluntary collective-bargaining tradition of organized labor and, until the 1970s, the opposition to codetermination of the Trade Union Congress. A more important factor, however, was the militancy and the jealously guarded independence of the shop steward movement. It was successful until Margaret Thatcher's rule in preventing worker participation from becoming structured, formalized, or contained by either union hierarchies or governmental stipulations. By controlling the organization of work on the shop floor and through the unpredictable use of wildcat strikes, shop steward organs were able to defy union leaders with impunity, at the same time that they could obstruct the productive process of industry and frustrate the main aims of government. Supported by their fellow rank-and-file unionists, shop stewards had the capacity—as demonstrated in 1979—to bring the nation to its knees. The source of both their power and their independence can be explained, in the first place, by the rigidity and ineptitude of the trade-union leadership. Over the years the shop stewards' committees—and there were 300,000 of them at the peak of their strength in the late 1960s—gradually replaced in their particular workplaces the union bureaucracy in setting the pay scales and work regulations through bargaining in a largely autonomous manner. Consequently, as J. H. Goldthorpe has pointed out, "the leverage that full-time officials can exert on the rank-and-file—the officials' ability to advise, guide, and persuade them into preferred courses of action—[was] greatly diminished."[59] Perhaps the gulf between the union leadership and the rank-and-file was reflected by the fact that more than 80 percent of the strikes in the pre-Thatcher postwar period were wildcat strikes called by the shop stewards.[60] In contrast to their counterparts on the continent, the top union leaders in England were slow to react to pressures from below; when they did respond, their actions tended to lack the vitality necessary for capturing the workers' allegiance.[61]

There is also a positive factor that accounts for the remarkable ability of shop stewards to sustain their influence over the rank and file and to retain their independence from the union bureaucracy. And that was the commitment—perhaps for pragmatic reasons—of most shop stewards to democracy as practiced on a regular basis on the shop floor. According to one student of industrial democracy:

> Through the shop stewards' movement, Britain has developed a unique layer of democratic trade unionism, which should be encouraged by every means. Although participation in union branches is often also as negligible as in other forms of political organization, at the work place level, where there is a real opportunity for effective influence on policy, participation is higher, and for example, in one study over 80 percent of workers reported regularly voting in shop-steward elections. Further, shop-stewards are normally obligated to be responsible to their members' wishes, or they are quickly replaced; there is, therefore, a fairly regular turnover of shop stewards, making experience of the role, and its responsibilities, widespread.[62]

Among working-class organs in industrial society, the shop steward movement in Britain must be ranked, from a democratic standpoint, as an important success. Since its inception in the years following World War I, however, the movement has never lived up to its potential as a working-class agency for social change. It has always accepted the basic structure and principles of capitalism, perhaps partly because workers recognized the superior power of employers, and partly because they were unable to break free from the hegemonic ideology of capitalism. Their focus was on maintaining control of the organization of work on the floor. Thus they were content to limit their bargaining to the range of issues that arose within the scope of their daily experience as workers.[63]

Moreover, the shop steward movement's approach even to these issues was profoundly apolitical. They viewed control of the shop floor as a way to enjoy personal freedom in industry. "This is not," wrote Goodrich, "identical with the demand for political power within industry; the one begins as a desire for no government, the other as a desire for a share in self-government."[64] This narrowness of vision not only inhibited their action but also obstructed their view of the source of the problem. "Limited to their own employer and organization," Clarke stated, workers "frequently fail to perceive the structural location of their problems in market and government demands; the real enemy is not the capitalist but the capitalist system of production."[65]

By the early 1970s the postwar economic boom in Britain had come to an end. This created an increase in the strike rate a well as a more deep-seated crisis in labor relations. Government, labor, and management all began to explore ways of resolving the crisis. The Trade Union Council began to modify its position on workers' participation. Traditionally it held that "collective bargaining and permanent opposition were the sole means of achieving industrial democracy."[66] By 1972 it argued that all large companies should be required to disclose a wide range of information to the unions and that union representatives should sit on company boards. In the elections of 1984 Labour pledged that if elected it would introduce an industrial democracy statute. Instead, it created a committee of inquiry to explore the matter further. The Bullock Report recommended, among other things, the enactment of a law requiring equal representation of workers and management on all large corporate boards. The business community reacted so vehemently against the Bullock proposals that it was reported as being "one of the most vitriolic and damning campaigns ever mounted by Britain's industrialists."[67] Captive of their traditional fear of the power of management cooptation, trade-union leaders could not generate much enthusiasm for the report. This allowed the Labor government to dodge the issue by creating yet another commission, which expeditiously and prudently suggested that firms need to retain their managerial prerogatives but should be obliged to establish Joint Representative Committees to facilitate discussions of items of mutual concern with workers. By 1980 these committees were well established in most large firms.

As for the usefulness of boardroom participation from the workers' perspective, Brannen points to an interesting paradox: "if worker representatives (on the board) are strong enough and willing to put forward competing rationalities they are likely to instigate decision-making moves elsewhere [e.g., by the financial committee of the board], thus rendering themselves impotent in the director role; but if they adopt the director role then their *raison d'être* . . . disappears."[68]

In the winter of 1978–79 a wave of wildcat strikes discredited the Labour government, and the Conservatives, with Margaret Thatcher at the helm, came to power determined above all else to curb the power of the unions.[69] In addition to legislatively bashing the miners in 1984–85, Thatcher was instrumental in passing four major union-busting bills. Particularly devastating for the unions was an act ascribing "legal personality" to unions themselves, which meant that more than just union officials could be sued for "illegal" activities. To put teeth into the act, the Tories enacted a vast array of restrictions that made unions increasingly vulnerable to legal action. Secondary actions were essentially banned, as were "political strikes"—walkouts over a government decision to close down a public agency. In addition, secret votes were required before a strike; picketing was tightly restricted; and the closed shop was, for all practical purposes, outlawed.[70]

Not only were the unions clobbered by the Tory government but they also suffered a political defeat stemming from the effort of leaders of the Labour party to break their traditionally close ties with the unions. In a policy statement the party leader Neil Kinnock asserted that trade unions are basically an interest group alongside all other interest groups and therefore should not play a decisive role in running the economy. Also, on the economic front the trade-union movement was hard hit by a decade of high unemployment and widespread deindustrialization. As a result, unions had lost one-fifth of their membership, wiping out the gains that they had made in the 1970s. Only 35 percent of the country's total workforce is now unionized, compared with a peak of 50 percent ten years ago.[71] The near-term potential for advances in worker participation in Britain, therefore, does not look good.

VI.   Inferences

What emerges from our brief account of the struggle for workplace democracy in western Europe in the postwar period is the presence of two major structural barriers to the democratization of the economy. The first and most forceful barrier is corporate power. As we have seen, when the issue is crucial to the interests of capital—as it was in Germany in relation to labor's demand for equal representation on corporate boards, and in Sweden concerning what was perceived to be the radicalness of the Meidner plan—business groups and their political allies are formidable defenders of the decision-making prerogatives of the private entrepreneur. The second major barrier to the transformation of workplace governance are trade unions. Traditionally, one of the principal functions of the union has been to negotiate collective-bargaining contracts and to enforce them. It is difficult to situate workplace democracy under either rubric defining the role of the union. In periods of rank-and-file unrest, however, union leaders uniformly undergo a radical transformation: They become militant in their stand for the extension of industrial democracy. However, in leading the struggle for this cause, the union invariably insists on two requirements that end up subverting the extension of democracy. First, unions advocate that any extension in "worker" participatory rights be registered legally, either in the form of a collective-bargaining contract or in a legislative statute, rather than being channeled in the form of de facto advancement in workers' rights, achieved and enforced by the workers themselves with backup support from the union. Second, unions contend that an extension in workers' participatory rights must be interpreted to mean an extension of union representation in the furtherance of workers' rights. The upshot of both union positions is that rank-and-file workers are discouraged from being the participatory agents themselves.

The proponents of workplace democracy are confronted by a serious dilemma: Progress toward achieving economic democracy is very much dependent upon well-organized, strong unions; yet there is an inherent contradiction between strong unions and industrial democracy. Some writers argue that the issue of workplace democracy must include the democratization of trade unions. The first step toward this goal is to persuade union leaders to favor workers rather than professional union representatives on company boards and in worker councils. Unfortunately, we are not informed how this task is to be accomplished. Other writers, in assuming that union leaders are disinclined to relinquish their power positions in these posts, argue that advancement in industrial democracy means, at best, that management autocracy is to be replaced by union decision making. In either case, the burden of the critique is that no matter what the nature of the advances in workplace democracy are, a sharp distinction is still being maintained between those who make the decisions and those who comply with them.[72] Put more forcefully, collective bargaining is condemned as a process "by which the rank and file, inferior in power, status, and treatment, are allowed to press for marginal improvements in their lot on condition that they leave unchallenged those structural features of the system which perpetuate their inferiority."[73]

In our view this perspective is overly pessimistic for two important reasons. In the first place, in measuring the progress toward economic democracy, it underestimates the difference between management autocracy as practiced in the pre-codetermination era and joint management-union decision making and consultation practiced within codetermination structures. Under the latter conditions, the responsibility of union representatives to protect workers' rights on a wide range of issues—from health, safety, and technological innovations to work schedules, organization of work, leaves of absence, plant closings, and the like—cannot but help stimulate workers' interest in plant or office affairs. The occasional contests that take place between workers and union officials for seats on the company board or the workers' council is indicative of this phenomenon.

Second, this pessimistic assessment focuses exclusively on the micro level—on the direct effect of codetermination and similar reforms on the lives of workers. In overlooking the macro level of politics, it misses the significant fact that during the postwar period—especially during the 1960s and 1970s—the issue of economic democracy often occupied center stage of the political arenas of most western European nations. These debates on an issue that directly relates to working people could not help but invigorate and expand the scope of the democratic process. They did this by focusing on a democratic issue which is central to the lives of working men and women. It involved and activated workers as participatory citizens and thus incorporated and refined their views concerning a common agenda of decision making for the entire polity. If, as seems apparent, socialism is becoming less of an issue in the 1990s, it is in the interest of democracy that other issues—harboring equally radical egalitarian consequences and being equally relevant and important to both workers and democracy—should emerge to replace it.

Moreover, as we have seen, a reinforcing participatory cycle developed during the postwar period as an outgrowth of labor's struggle for economic democracy. It is a cycle that may continue to function as a supportive process for democratic politics. This political cycle is characterized by (1) rank-and-file worker unrest and protest, which (2) spurs the radicalization of trade unions which in order to regain the loyalty of workers, (3) generate political struggle, demanding the advancement of economic democracy through legislation or collective bargaining or both. (4) Success in this endeavor tends in time to reestablish the insensitivity of the union bureaucracy and leadership toward the concerns and needs of the rank and file. But this insensitivity in turn creates rank-and-file unrest and protest, which reactivates the cycle. Significantly, each cyclical process has expanded workers' participatory rights beyond what was achieved in previous cycles.

Although the issue of worker participation declined, if it did not totally disappear, in the 1980s—a period that was marked by a strong political swing to the right—one can hope that the participatory cycles so evident in the 1960s and 1970s will reemerge when the left regains power. If indeed they do reemerge, the left should strive to be in a sounder position theoretically to sustain and expand the democratic potential of these participatory cycles.

Workplace Democracy
in America

5

Worker participation is substantially less developed and widespread in postwar America than in European countries; it came into being comparatively late, in the 1970s, and then only because of the initiative of management. The anemic state of worker participation in American industry is not surprising, given the weakness of the trade-union movement. As we have seen from the European experience, in spite of the tensions subsisting between trade-union bureaucracy and worker participation, advancement toward greater worker participation very much depends upon a strong labor movement. The failure of business elites to accept trade unions as legitimate actors in the economy and in politics contributed significantly to the stunting of worker participation in American industry. To the extent, however, that worker participation has developed—largely under the tutelage of business—it has generated, we will argue, a dialectical process that has considerable potential to nurture the beginnings of a democratically conceived participatory movement across the

American workplace as a whole. The sharp decline in union membership and power since the 1980s does not, as one might expect, lessen this potential. On the contrary, in fomenting a crisis within the labor movement, it may have increased it.

I

Quality of work life (QWL) programs began in the late 1960s and early 1970s in response to capital's search for a way to combat chronically low productivity. As became evident in the "Lordstown" breakthrough in modern technology, younger, better-educated workers were increasingly less willing to tolerate mind-killing, dehumanizing work despite increasing wage rates. Their anger and frustration was expressed in wildcat strikes, absenteeism, sabotage, tardiness, turnover, and the like. Numerous workers complained chiefly about jobs that provided no mental challenge and allowed for insufficient worker control over job assignments. In a survey, workers were asked "whether it was a good idea for corporations in America to become more like they are in Europe, in offering workers more involvement in corporate governance." In 1976, 50 percent said yes; by 1979, it was 74 percent.[1]

QWL has taken many forms, but most generally it consists of a program where workers meet once a week in groups of ten to fifteen in problem-solving sessions to identify, analyze, and solve problems. QWL's have no direct power—being restricted by management's judgment of what constitutes an admissible problem and solution, and, when a union contract is in force, by the collective-bargaining agreement. But within these bounds, their influence has been substantial. Judged by their popularity among management, they have increased productivity by lowering absenteeism and increasing worker morale. According to a 1982 survey conducted by the New York Stock Exchange, 75 percent of all U.S. corporations with more than 10,000 employees had a QWL program.[2] In 1981

Business Week declared that QWL programs had ushered in a "New Industrial Relations" within which "the U.S. industrial relations system, so long arrested at primitive levels, can now evolve into a . . . participative stage."[3]

In the early 1980s a second generation of participatory programs was spurred by international competition, emanating especially from Japan and West Germany, which had already developed, as we have seen, far more effective schemes of worker participation than were prevalent in the United States. These programs went beyond the problem-solving orientation of the QWL program to more extensive forms of participation, including job rotation, payment for increased skills and knowledge, and autonomous work teams. The radical feature of these programs was the ceding to workers of a considerable measure of shop-floor control in exchange for an increased commitment by workers to their jobs and the firm. They thereby institutionalized a limited but nonetheless identifiable economic arena within which democratic participation plays a legitimate role.

In more than a few cases workers' enthusiasm for self-rule has encroached on domains deemed "management prerogatives," creating sharp worker-management tensions.[4] However, management is usually able to curb worker participatory advances before they reach the confrontation point. As one observer of autonomous work groups put it, "after an initial round of success, [workers] reach a 'plateau,' and are discouraged at every turn from proceeding to more ambitious projects."[5]

Corporate managers could not help but be aware of the ideological and strategic risk involved in their sponsoring worker participatory programs.[6] For example, top managers at General Motors voiced the fear that allowing workers to participate in shop-floor decisions would set the stage for their calling into question the prerogatives of management altogether.[7] A participatory project at Polaroid was stopped, according to a

Polaroid official, because "it was too successful. What were we going to do with the supervisors—the managers? We didn't need them anymore. Management decided that it didn't want operators that qualified. The employees' newly revealed ability to carry more responsibility was too great a threat to the established way of doing things and to established power patterns."[8]

These concerns of some firms, however, were generally overshadowed by businesses that recognized that the mass-production paradigm was obsolete, unable to meet the imperatives of advanced technology, and thus disqualified from successfully surmounting the challenge of international competition. The most effective utilization of the new and emerging technologies called for an integrative and flexible work force; a participatory system in which autonomous work groups allocate work themselves, often ignoring job classifications, seniority rules, and supervisory jurisdictions. The success of autonomous work programs was predicated upon management's acknowledgment of the changing contours of the capitalist labor process, which now requires worker integration as assuredly as earlier it had assigned priority to worker subordination to management authority, and that given the evolution of industrial technology, worker integration could serve as the functional equivalent of that subordination.[9]

II

The nature of the relationship, if any, between employee ownership and worker participation is a disputed issue. It is an important issue since the growth of employee-owned firms during the past two decades has been substantial, and it is likely that it will continue to grow as the economy declines. More than 7,000 firms covering 10 million employees are estimated to have some degree of employee ownership. Although workers own less than half of the stock in most employee-owned firms, several hundred of these firms are majority employee-owned.[10] The Employee Stock Ownership Plan, or ESOP, is the most popular form of employee ownership. ESOP, a creation of Congress, is designed to encourage workers to own stock in the company in which they work. And, owing to their generous tax benefits, ESOPs are attractive to corporations. In addition to ESOPs, Congress has established several agencies, including the National Consumer Cooperative Bank, the Economic Development Administration, and the Small Business Administration, whose agendas include the facilitating of the formation of worker cooperatives and worker buyouts.[11]

The democratic critics of employee-owned firms contend that there is little relationship between employee ownership and worker participation. The data appears to bear out their contention. Although the great majority of employee-owned firms have some form of worker participation, only a small minority of them provide for worker participation in policy questions beyond the shop floor.[12] "The mere presence of worker ownership," Joseph Blasi states, "leads to very little new cooperation and certainly not to [worker] control." He found that even in companies in which workers have a majority ownership, they have not taken the initiative to assert their right to participate. "Employee owners often feel that ownership has no real meaning for them. . . . The organization of the firm empties employee ownership of its substance."[13] It is also argued that there is widespread exclusion of lower-paid workers from ownership in ESOP firms. As a result, it is claimed that ESOPs tend to "freeze out" or dampen shop-floor worker participation.[14]

Democratic proponents of employee ownership point to the results of recent studies that find that those firms which combine worker ownership *with* a strong worker-participation program outperformed conventional and other employee-owned firms in improving productivity and raising job satisfaction. Not only does employee ownership provide favorable psychological conditions for the promotion of effective worker participation, but it is also suggested that employee ownership

acts as a legal barrier against management's unilaterally re-
voking a participatory program.[15] The linkage of participation
with worker ownership legitimates workers' participation as
a property right that workers, as owners, are entitled to. To
conceptualize participation as a property right has the political advantage of deradicalizing the issue of workplace democracy. Rather than being identified with a radical interpretation of democracy or socialism, worker participation, it is
argued, can now be subsumed under the traditional panoply
of rights protected by the Constitution.[16] This "conservative"
argument for worker participation, however, has remained,
at least until now, a nonissue. Large corporations that have
been "bought out" by their employees, such as the Avis Corporation, have been organized along traditional, hierarchical
lines.

III

Worker-participation programs have
also been established as an antiunion device. This device has
been shown to be extremely effective in keeping unions out. A
1977 survey indicated that nonunion workers who participated
in worker-participation programs were less likely to respond
to appeals for union representation than the average worker.
A more recent study has found that three-fourths of the companies facing white-collar organizing drives have established
some sort of employee committee to help in their defense. The
most startling finding along these lines is from an AFL-CIO
survey of organizing campaigns. This survey found that the
most effective counterstrategy that companies could employ to
discredit and demoralize union organizing drives was to institute a QWL plan, especially in manufacturing establishments.
Unions won only 8 percent of the organizational campaigns in
companies with QWL plans, as opposed to 36 percent in these
industries overall.[17] IBM, General Electric, and General Foods

are among the large corporations that have made heavy use of worker participation to avoid unionization. Both General Electric and General Foods have stated that work-improvement programs were integral to their antiunion campaigns.[18]

Charles Heckscher, a leading scholar in labor relations, warns that this evidence should not make one overly pessimistic concerning the value of worker-participation programs. He points out that when a union is actively involved in the worker participatory process, it *strengthens,* rather than weakens, the union. In support of his contention, he cites various studies that show that there is a correlation between union support of QWL programs and rank-and-file commitment to the union.[19] He also points out that not only have the heads of the three largest unions, United Automobile Workers, Communications Workers of America, and the United Steelworkers of America, become active advocates of worker-participation programs, but that the AFL-CIO, after years of opposition, changed its position in 1985 in support of worker-participation programs. It stated that

the survey data suggest, and our experience indicates, that there is a particular insistence voiced by workers, union and nonunion alike, to have a say in the "how, why, and wherefore" of their work. These needs and desires are being met in some cases by union-management programs affording greater worker participation in decisionmaking at the workplace. Several major unions have developed such programs and report a positive membership response. The labor movement should seek to accelerate this development.[20]

Heckscher's position is not entirely convincing. No major union has joined the participatory ranks since 1985. This is understandable in light of the declaration of war by corporate elites against unionism in recent years. In an atmosphere of management-labor mistrust, it is problematic, at best, that a participatory program strengthens the union. Traditionally, the trade-union movement both in the United States and in Europe has been ambivalent, if not hostile, to participatory schemes. Union critics of worker-participation structures argue that their very nature violates both the letter and spirit of collective-bargaining contracts. They contend that the abolition of clearly defined job structures, pay scales, promotion standards, seniority rights, supervisory duties, and other collective-bargaining arrangements strips the union of much of its legal power to enforce the rules. Furthermore, they argue, worker participation renders the union vulnerable to the twin dangers of fragmentation and manipulation. When workers are directly authorized to do what they do by union authorities, they constitute a cohesive unit occupying an oppositional stance in relation to management. When workers participate in shopfloor decisions, differences of opinion between them have an opportunity to grow and develop, and many of them give vent to their traditional predilection of following management, which interacts with them much more closely on a day-to-day basis than does the union. During periods of negotiations between union and management, these centrifugal tendencies become all the more pronounced and disruptive of union organizational plans.[21] Moreover, it is pointed out, that by providing channels of mobility and leadership, participatory structures can become cooptative for even some of the more militant among the rank and file. In sum, the critics of participatory programs argue that because of the unequal resources in favor of management, these programs are fundamentally biased against both workers and unions.[22]

William Winpisinger, president of the International Association of Machinists and Aerospace Workers, summarized the case against QWL and similar programs forcefully:

> Through manipulation and rigged committees, workers find themselves subject to speedups, unsafe working conditions, or divisive peer-group pressure. . . . QWL programs often result

in significant cost savings for the company. Will workers benefit from these savings? . . . It is both unreasonable and unfair to ask workers to engage in problem-solving to improve the operations of the company unless their own jobs are protected. Why don't we follow the Japanese on this score—who almost always guarantee job security, etc. . . . Corporate America can hardly expect us to cooperate in these efforts while they simultaneously fund and support a so-called union-free environment movement dedicated to our destruction.[23]

IV

Although Winpisinger makes his case forcefully, the rejection of worker-participation programs, despite their threat to unions, is not a tenable option for the American labor movement. As we have seen from the AFL-CIO statement and as documented by numerous surveys, workers like direct participation. More importantly, from the standpoint of management, extensive studies have shown significant correlation between increased worker participation and reduced absenteeism and turnover, and improved labor productivity.[24] Thus, it is likely that participatory programs are here to stay. For unions to write them off as instruments of "union busting" is to allow management to preempt the field and consequently be in a position to increase employee commitment to the firm.

However, as the phenomenon of the "plateau" demonstrates, the inherent contradiction between worker participation and management authority is also latently present in these programs and should not be overlooked by unions. This contradiction is most evident in the more successful autonomous work teams, which generate increased work competence and higher morale and commitment to the job and the firm. However, work activity of this kind also fosters greater self-confidence and feelings of empowerment among workers, leading them to demand greater autonomy and responsibility. Almost inevitably this gives rise to management constraints upon worker control, which in turn engender worker frustration and dissatisfaction. An empirical study of autonomous work teams documents precisely this dynamic of participation that nurtures workers' feelings and the reality, to a limited extent, of greater empowerment. This sense of empowerment in turn provokes management to infringe upon workers' decision-making authority, which disillusions them and destabilizes the rationale that motivated management to support the worker-participation plan in the first place.[25] John Witte and others note that almost all workers who have engaged in participatory programs, especially the more educated and the more active in participatory programs, desire more participation than they are allowed.[26]

V

Parallel to the structural contradiction between management authority and workplace democracy there exists a structural contradiction between worker participation and collective-bargaining contracts. The dual structure of direct worker participation and representative collective bargaining serves as both a barrier and a spur to the extension of worker participatory rights: As a barrier since worker participation is seen by both management and union as a potential threat to their respective spheres of authority; and as a spur since they are both under pressure—management to increase productivity, and organized labor to maintain the allegiance of its members—to support worker participatory programs.

It is fortunate from the perspective of the proponents of workplace democracy that no structural contradictions exist between advanced technology and worker participation. On the contrary, "technology" and "participation" are harmonious concepts, each working to reinforce and strengthen the other. With the evolution of new technology, management loses its monopoly concerning how to produce high-quality, competitive products. This knowledge is now diffused within the workforce as a whole, thus calling upon a range of employees to join with management in making daily judgments requisite to the application of the new technology, provide quality control, and establish new patterns of labor-management relations that enhance morale and productivity within the firm.[27] The congeniality, indeed, the dependency, of technology on the flexible, problem-solving, creativity-engendering capacity of a participatory workplace is well expressed by Carmen Sirianni:

> Participatory sociotechnical systems, especially when combined with the informating potential of the new technologies, allow for multiskilling and permanent learning that cut across old demarcations, and often involve an understanding of the entire process of production. Workers' horizons become broader, and their skills more theoretical or intellective. Tacit, embodied, and often exclusive skills become more explicit, public, and shared. Technology itself becomes a tool for learning and exercising discretion, and information systems become more open and less blocked by hierarchical controls. And the theoretical skills learned to run one kind of informated process are often applicable to a variety of other areas of production, service, and administration as well.[28]

Despite the emerging dependency of new technologies on workplace democracy, organized labor has failed to exploit this new development for its own advantage. Instead, there is practically unanimous agreement among labor leaders that for worker participatory programs to be legitimate, they must be institutionalized within collective-bargaining agreements. An even more favorable arrangement, as they see it, is one in which the union formally participates in joint management-labor committees.[29] As we have seen in European countries, these kinds of arrangements have created tensions between rank and file desirous of participating in workplace decision making and union representatives who want to restrict the participatory process to issues that do not encroach upon the collective-bargaining contract.

According to Kochan, "less than a majority of union members rate their union as performing well on QWL issues."[30] Another study reports that unions are "accepted as counter-bureaucracies necessary for self-protection but hardly valuable in themselves."[31] Most revealing of union resistance to worker-participation programs is Heckscher's observation that the union's restrictive role in limiting the scope of worker autonomy has been substantial, that it has acted to police rather than to develop worker participation. The same indictment can be made against the European union bureaucracies.[32]

VI

It seems apparent to us that organized labor cannot maintain its cautious, do-nothing stance on the issue of workplace democracy and expect to survive as a trade-union movement. What is called for is a bold strategy in which unions are prepared to renounce their exclusive dependence on collective-bargaining contracts and instead openly embrace the fluidity implicit in their seeking to provide appropriate leadership in the struggle to democratize the workplace setting itself.[33] The motive force behind such a strategy is that it harbors the potential to rekindle commitment and loyalty among union members and thereby provide a solid basis for restoring union power and status. As we have seen, this strategy was adopted successfully from time to time by European trade unions to bolster their declining power. Admittedly, this commitment lasted as long as union power was directed toward the protection and extension of worker participation. When that effort was no longer forthcoming, the loyalty weakened and was eventually broken. The reemergence of distance and tension between workers and unions again triggered unions to resume their struggle for worker participation, and thus to reestablish the connection between workers' commitment and union power. As we have seen, this recurring cycle in postwar Europe made some progress—despite the unions' insistence on controlling the participatory system—toward the extension of worker participatory rights. More importantly, it was a process that invigorated democracy. It is this process which America urgently needs to initiate. Clearly, it will not come into being until organized labor is prepared to fight for workers' participatory rights and thereby for its own life.

There are two major risks deterring labor from engaging in such a battle at this time. The most obvious one is that, given their declining and decrepit state, the unions are no match for the power of the corporations. This issue will be dealt with in the next chapter. Here we want to discuss the other risk, namely, that a struggle for workplace democracy might turn out to be too successful in that workers, as distinguished from union officials, might actually gain decision-making powers. If this were to occur, would not workers' loyalty and commitment to the union, nurtured during the struggle to obtain worker participation, begin to wane once participatory structures and rights were firmly established? Would not the unions' victory in obtaining worker participatory rights undermine its own power in the long run?

As long as it continues to make sense to demarcate between the power of management and the power of workers, that is, as long as a worker-participatory system has not been fully democratized, such a fear seems unjustified. For under present conditions, which undoubtedly will remain operative for the foreseeable future, union power must be relied on by workers to enforce the existing, although incomplete, participatory system and rules that are in place and to extend and improve them over time.

Unions should be primarily concerned, in other words, with

the enforcement, improvement, and extension of the democratic process of decision making in the workplace, rather than investing their major energies, as they are at present, with policing substantive regulations regarding wage scales, working conditions, and the like. Therefore, unlike the structural contradiction between managerial authority and worker participation, there is no *inherent* contradiction between union power and worker participation as long as a power differential remains—either under capitalism or socialism or both—between management and workers. As long as management continues to maintain its oppositional stance to workers, there is no good reason for unions to conceive of workplace democracy as a basic threat to their power. On the contrary, the underlying fact, which is ignored by unions only at their peril, is that under modern technological conditions in industry and in offices, unions' essential source of power turns on their commitment and ability to further the cause of workplace democracy.

Power and Utopia

6

I

A growing number of scholars acknowledge that workplace democracy is an essential next step in the struggle for democracy.[1] Robert Dahl, for example, argues, "We . . . see no convincing reason why we should not exercise our right to the democratic process in the government of enterprises, just as we have already done in the government of the states. And we intend to exercise that right."[2] On the crucial issue of how to gain recognition of this right—that is, how to achieve workplace democracy, or even how to progress toward its realization—Dahl and other like-minded theorists have come up with barren strategies for change. Democratic theorists are thus confronted with a daunting paradox: As workplace democracy becomes more accepted as an essential democratic goal, it simultaneously becomes more elusive, unattainable, and utopian.

This utopianism is well illustrated in Dahl's influential book *A Preface to Economic Democracy*. In his brief concluding section on "Transition," he states that "a system of self-governing enterprises along the lines I have sketched would, I believe, appeal to a people committed to equality with liberty."[3] In effect, Dahl regards his function, indeed his obligation, as a committed democrat and political scientist as having been fulfilled. Having made his case for industrial democracy, it is now up to the people to decide. He has discharged his scholarly responsibility and articulated his democratic vision. He can do no more.

In our view Dahl has not fully exercised his responsibility as a democrat and as a political scientist. Implementation of workplace democracy would require a massive redistribution of power against the vested interests of corporate elites. It appears somewhat naive to suggest that this will occur by simply putting the case before the people, as Dahl has suggested. An issue of this magnitude is likely to reach the agenda for democratic decision making only in response to organized, sustained, and massive political pressure generated by demonstrations, marches, strikes, boycotts, and the like. Congress would never have considered, much less passed, the Wagner Act, which unprecedentedly established collective bargaining as an instrument of national policy, if the enactment had not been preceded by prolonged and widespread class struggle. Yet the issues of that time—in terms of their impact upon the redistribution of power—would be dwarfed by a proposal to democratize corporate power structures. Similarly, it is doubtful whether the Civil Rights Act of 1964 would have been passed had Martin Luther King, Jr., and his colleagues failed to gain a broad spectrum of national support through their power struggle with "Bull" Connor and his fellow segregationists.

By ignoring the power issue inherent in the implementation of his proposal, Dahl avoids dealing with the issue of class struggle as a democratic means for social change. Had he at least recognized the problem of implementation and considered, on the basis of past historical evidence, the legitimacy of class struggle as an appropriate means to expand and strengthen democracy, his proposal would have had more bite. Such a declaration by Dahl and other intellectuals could serve as a catalyst—similar to that of the Supreme Court's *Brown* decision on the civil rights movement—stirring labor to mount a broad-based struggle for the democratization of industry. However, by not accepting this challenge, he has in effect depoliticized the issue of workplace democracy. With participation removed from the real world of power, no basic interests are threatened; workplace democracy becomes devoid of practical meaning and, at best, becomes a utopian ideal or management ploy.

Benjamin Barber's *Strong Democracy* is another work in a similar vein that also comes to a dead end. Although he strongly advocates workplace democracy, together with other participatory institutions—such as a proposed national initiative and referendum—when it comes to implementation the argument ends in a whimper. Barber warns that if any of his proposals, including workplace democracy, is adopted piecemeal, the participatory project would become counterproductive. "They must be adopted together or not at all."[4] But given the fragmentary nature of American politics, the chances that Barber's proposals would be considered as a unit—much less adopted wholesale—are minuscule. Again, the issue of participatory democracy is relegated to a utopian status.

II

Other participationists, such as Carole Pateman and Ronald Mason, believe that involvement in the participatory process over an extended period of time will develop the psychological, social, and political capacities of participants and thus deepen and broaden their understanding of and commitment to democracy. They argue that even a piecemeal participatory experience in pseudo-democratic surroundings tends to stimulate further participation, leading in a contagious way from one enterprise and institution to another. From this gradual and nonconfrontational process the beginnings of a participatory society are expected to emerge. Class struggle accordingly has no role to play in promoting such a society. Since class struggle is gratuitous, its legitimacy becomes, at best, an academic issue.

This position, in our view, is theoretically flawed in two important respects: It conceives of democracy exclusively as process and thus ignores whether the outcomes of the process are democratic; and democracy is viewed in micro terms, disregarding the possible ideological impact upon macro politics of the outcomes of micro "democratic" processes. This one-dimensional conceptualization of democracy can in practice result in an untenable position of endorsing, as democratic, decisions whose outcomes are antithetical to such fundamental democratic values as the equal worth of all persons. Critics of this conception of democratic participation invariably question, for example, how a "participatory" political community that seeks to exclude Jews and blacks could conceivably be regarded as democratic. These critics argue that democratic participation is not only compatible with, but is often conducive to, the most radically antidemocratic outcomes.

However, this criticism is justified only because most versions of participatory theory are deficiently formulated, since they focus on process and the micro level of politics to the neglect of ends and the macro implications for democracy. Carole Pateman, for example, defines democratic participation as "a process where each individual member of a decision-making body has equal power to determine the outcome of decisions," and where "the whole body of employees in each enterprise makes management decisions." This "would mean that the present distinction between management, permanently in office, and the men, permanent subordinates, was abolished."[5] A primary consequence of defining democratic participation exclusively in terms of process and procedure, ignoring ends, is to downgrade the value of and commitment to democracy. For when democracy is conceptualized in this one-dimensional way, we are confronted with the irreconcilable dilemma of a democratic process producing an unacceptable undemocratic outcome.

It would accord better with our common-sense intuitions, as well as make the theory of democracy less vulnerable to attack, if it were conceptualized as comprising both means and ends: the principal end being the self-development of all individuals in the participatory and not the possessively individualist sense defined above, and the chief means to that end being equal and effective citizen participation at all levels of public decision making. The core principle embodied in both ends and means is the equality of worth of individuals. Ends and means conjoined in this way would preclude any query about the participatory exclusion of minorities, for political means that produced undemocratic ends could not be claimed to be authentically democratic means.

Democratically conceived, means and ends can never be rendered totally distinct. This is so because the means themselves are never independent of the ends but only constitute their embodiment at a particular moment in time. The means just is the end at a particular stage in time, and needs to be democratically assessed in those terms. Thus, when a participatory decision-making group of whites seeks to exclude blacks from its participatory community, it violates not only the ends of democracy but the means as well. For means are in effect a foreshortened version of ends.

Pateman defines democratic worker participation as "a process where each individual member of a decision-making body has equal power to determine the outcome of decisions." This is a sound definition except that it limits participation to the micro level and appears oblivious of the impact of societywide forces upon micro participatory structures. It would hardly be convincing to hold that workers' decisions on major issues were democratically arrived at if they were dictated, directly or indirectly, by outside trade-union, governmental, or business elites. Similarly, it would not be reasonable to claim that these decisions were democratically reached to the extent that they were shaped by a societally imposed ideology. Such "participation," notwithstanding its form, is more repressive than democratic. Pateman's unfortunately narrow view precludes a proper sensitivity to the impact of an inequalitarian and class-bound society upon workers' decisions in an ostensibly democratic workplace.

Her definition of pseudo- or partial participation also misses the mark. She describes it as occurring when workers "are in the unequal position of permanent subordinates: the final prerogative of decision-making rests with the permanent superiors, with management."[6] This definition is too broad because, under some conditions and in certain contexts, what Pateman calls pseudo-participation is in reality genuine worker participation. This would be the case, for example, when workers gain a partial, though significant, foothold in the enterprise over management's opposition. Such a modest victory would not qualify under Pateman's definition of democratic participation but could well raise workers' consciousness and spur them on to greater efforts. Moreover, it could also serve as a model for workers elsewhere in their struggle for participatory rights. The link between the micro and macro levels can most effectively be forged when participation becomes a vehicle for workers in their successful struggle for power, no matter how limited the initial victories might be.

Under other circumstances, Pateman's concept of pseudo-participation seems too narrow because it could easily accommodate a form of repressive participation. This would obtain when workers engage in managerially planned participatory programs that, unbeknown to themselves, increased management control over their working lives.

The existence of repressive participation, although not identified as such, is frequently reported in the literature on workplace democracy. For example, Michael Poole concludes that "in the bulk of experiments in industrial democracy developed so far . . . the role of managers, far from being severely circumscribed, has actually been considerably enhanced."[7] Similarly, Arnold Tannenbaum argues, "Workers who have some sense of control in most of the organizations we have studied are in general more or less positively disposed towards their supervisors and managers."[8] A 1979 Trilateral Commission report observes that worker-participation programs enhance managerial legitimacy and perhaps lessen the dependence of workers on unions. Not surprisingly, the National Association of Manufacturers suggests that participatory structures can be used to sustain a "union-free environment."[9]

The gradualist optimism that pervades Pateman's analysis of micro structures of participation is unjustified for reasons analogous to our critique of the traditionally formulated means-end distinction and the micro-macro distinction. By conceptualizing participatory democracy largely in "process" terms, Pateman has no means of evaluating the democratic import of ongoing participatory structures. Outside of a context of continuing assessment in relation to the democratic ends of self-development of all individuals together with a growing commitment to the well-being of the participatory community, participation can lead to an intensification of competitive, anti-democratic outcomes.

Edward Greenberg, in his well-known and insightful critique of workplace democracy,[10] errs in much the same way as Pateman. For although he recognizes the impact of macro forces on those participating in the micro process, he does not consider the effect of the attitudes of workers on the nature of the political process in which they as decision makers participate. Thus, his position permits a political process to be characterized as democratic even while producing consistently antidemocratic results. Like Pateman, Greenberg conceptualizes democracy exclusively in terms of process or means.

On the basis of observation and data from interviews and questionnaires in fourteen plywood cooperatives in the Northwest, Greenberg found that despite the cooperative, democratic, and equalitarian relationships that workers experienced in the workplace, with respect to the outside world their outlook remained fully attached to values that best served to maximize "possessive individualism." Ironically "the democratic process," in Greenberg's eyes, actually reinforced the worker's bonds to their individualized, competitive values. In Greenberg's words: "The overwhelming impression from the data is that the experience of self-management within enterprises oriented to sales in a competitive marketplace is to enhance and nurture the small-property petit-bourgeois orientation that shareholders bring with them upon joining." [11] More specifically, the workers' participatory experience in these firms "nurtured attitudes that were basically inconsistent with such democratic values as community, equality, and confidence in others." [12]

He therefore argues that it is sheer speculation to believe that, within the context of capitalism, democratic worker-managed enterprises will generate large-scale democratic change. In effect, the experience of workplace democracy is no match for the educative power of the market. [13]

Greenberg concludes that workplace democracy, though an admirable idea, cannot be effective unless integrated into a broader socialist program for change. "The bright promise of workplace democracy and self-management can be achieved only if it is a part of a larger struggle for popular democracy and equality in the United States." [14] By insisting that workplace democracy has political relevance only in a revolutionary context, Greenberg has relegated the relevance of "workplace democracy"—albeit for different reasons than those adduced by Pateman, Dahl, and Barber—to a distant future. Thus, in effect, workplace democracy has once again been relegated to the realm of utopia.

In conceiving democracy solely from the perspective of process, ignoring the interaction of means and ends, Greenberg understandably believes that the worker cooperatives that he studied are "truly self-governing institutions and not what some would call partial or pseudo-participatory institutions." [15] However, when his conception of democracy is juxtaposed to a broader conception, one that encompasses ends as well as processes, the conclusion is inescapable that the "democratic process" engaged in by the workers at the plywood cooperatives was tainted by a strong dose of repressiveness. Its repressiveness is evidenced by the fact that the outcomes of the participatory process nurture attitudes that are antithetical to such democratic ends as individual equality and dignity. In essence, Greenberg's study can be viewed as an in-depth analysis of repressive worker participation.

Indeed, he may be right that democratically controlled enterprises cannot effect social change or overcome prevalent market values. However, his study throws no light on the issue, since, in misconceiving the concept of democracy, he ends up studying—unbeknown to himself—antidemocratic rather than democratic enterprises.

More importantly, because of his flawed conception of democracy, he is unable to adequately formulate and explore the key question: To what extent can workplace democracy, as a principal demand for power by a working-class movement, provoke social change within a liberal capitalist society?

More broadly stated, Greenberg fails to examine the question of whether present conditions in the United States are conducive to the development of a working-class movement when workplace democracy is conceived, not as a string of cooperative enterprises congenial to the ongoing economic order, but as a series of working-class demands geared toward the democratization of the workplace.

Within the context of a multidimensional conception of democracy—which stresses macro as well as micro orientations, ends as well as processes—we envision the possibility that workplace democracy can become an effective democratic demand, notwithstanding an inhospitable environment, when it is directed as a counterhegemonic force against corporate oligarchy.

It is the viability of this contention, and issues relating to it, that we are exploring in this book.

III

As we have seen, a growing number of democratic theorists recognize that workplace democracy is the foremost issue on the democratic political agenda. Although they strongly advocate the adoption of industrial democracy, they have uniformly shied away from confronting the question of how this fundamental democratic reform can be transformed into reality. This avoidance is manifested primarily as a refusal to deal with strategies of social change—as though this subject is of no concern to democratic theorists—and by adhering to an excessively narrow and one-dimensional view of democracy. This avoidance has shielded democratic theorists from confronting a key question: Should class struggle—struggle that is initiated from below—be regarded as an integral and, at times, a crucial element in the democratic process? It is surprising that despite the rich history of working-class struggle in America, theorists have persistently neglected this issue. Thus, class struggle has been circumvented as a democratically legitimate way to foster social change. As a result, the analyst who is concerned to promote workplace democracy is left with a choice among three barren alternatives: The issue must be left for the people as a whole to take the initiative; worker participation will evolve naturally from isolated "democratic" enterprises to encompass industry as a whole; and workplace democracy must await socialism before it can be instituted. These are the dismal options that have ensured that workplace democracy is confined to a utopian status.

Public and Private Space:
A Democratic Perspective

7

I

The major concepts of the public in contemporary political theory—liberal, neoclassical, and participationist—are beset by paradoxes that carry contradictory implications for democratic theory. We first formulate as clearly as possible the nature of these paradoxes and show how they build upon one another. We then suggest an approach for avoiding these paradoxes and proceed to state what a more coherent conception of the public within democratic theory—and its implementation within a democratic society—might look like.

As conceived by classical liberalism, society is divided into two spheres: the civil (or private) and the political (or public). The primacy of the civil sphere is stressed, for it is here that all members of society, each with his or her own aims, interests, and ambitions, have free space to strive toward their goals. To protect this arena of freedom from encroachment, "liberty of conscience" and the "right of private action" have become the principal functions of the political. This sphere is conceived in

instrumental terms and evokes the image of a necessary evil
to be tolerated to the extent that it enables individuals to pursue their private ends. Thus rational persons, as Robert Dahl
once insisted, participate in politics only when it is likely that
their involvement will yield private benefits beyond the cost of
political participation.[1]

There is another strand in liberal thought, from Rousseau to
John Dewey and the present. It argues that owing to the separation in life between private and public spheres, individuals
are obliged to act in a "dual capacity": as private persons to
maximize their selfish interests, and as public persons, as citizens in public space, to strive for the common good. However,
as Dewey admits, citizens "still have their private interests to
serve and interests of special groups, those of family, clique
or class to which they belong."[2] Dewey's fear that the public
realm could not withstand the invasion of private interest was
soon graphically confirmed by Harold Lasswell's choice of the
title for his early classic *Politics, Who Gets What, When and How?*
The starkness of Lasswell's title highlights the indifference of
political scientists as to whether policy outcomes are the result
of selfish interests or public concerns. This same indifference
is reflected in David Easton's well-known conception of the
political system as that which relates to the "authoritative allocation of values for a society."[3] Under this formulation of the
political system, outcomes are equally authoritative whether
they are a product of private or public interests. Thus the paradox: The concept of the public is a formal necessity in liberal
theory that has institutionally been susceptible to privatization
from within.

A familiar way to resolve this liberal paradox of the public is
to broaden the conception of the public. Instead of regarding
the public good merely as the outcome of competition among
private interests and their public spokesmen, Hannah Arendt,
Sheldon Wolin, and others have argued that the public is that
which relates to common concerns.[4] Politics from this perspective has a broadening and enriching effect upon citizen

participants who determine through their participation what the common good is. For both Arendt and Wolin, what distinguishes the public is not solely that the decision reached is in the common good, but that it is an outgrowth of participatory political action by citizens. In Wolin's words, politics in public space is "an integrative experience which brings together the multiple role-activities of the contemporary person and demands that the separate roles be surveyed from a more general point of view. It means further that efforts be made to restore the political art as that art which strives for an integrative form of direction."[5] This kind of integrative action is in sharp contrast to present interest-group politics, which Arendt regards as a "perverted form of 'acting together' " by actors "who know nothing and can do nothing."[6] With deep admiration for the distinct and majestic Greek *polis,* Arendt writes: "their freedom was not an inner realm into which men might escape at will from the pressures of the world. . . . Freedom for them could exist only in public; it was a tangible, worldly reality, something created by men to be enjoyed by men rather than a gift or a capacity, it was the man-made public space which antiquity had known as the area where freedom appears and becomes visible to all."[7]

By underscoring the importance of public freedom and public happiness, Arendt departs fundamentally from the Lockian-American commitment to private liberty and private happiness. Because of their crucial mistake in reversing public and private priorities, liberal societies, she argues, have essentially deprived their citizens of freedom.[8] Along similar lines, Wolin argues that the recent trend to politicize nonpolitical groups is to "deprive citizenship of its meaning and to render political loyalty impossible."[9] What has emerged from this trend is "a series of tight little islands, each evolving toward political self-sufficiency, each striving to absorb the individual members, each without any natural affiliations with a more comprehensive unity."[10]

True to the spirit of the Greek *polis,* both theorists vigorously support citizen participation in the determination of public policy. In a radical vein, Arendt claims that a representative system of government is inherently oligarchic even when it is assumed that governmental policy outcomes are in the real interest of the many. It is oligarchic in the sense that the many are relegated to a role of passivity while the privileged few engage in the pursuit of "public happiness and public freedom."[11] As we have seen, Wolin believes that involvement in public affairs provides citizens with an integrative and enriching experience that is unattainable in all other spheres of human activity.[12]

Also like the Greeks—who excluded women, slaves, and other noncitizens from public participation—both Arendt and Wolin hold to an exclusionary position. Arendt asserts that since "the obvious inability and conspicuous lack of interest of large parts of the population in political matters" is a reality of life, public business should be shared by "those few from all walks of life who have a taste for public freedom and cannot be 'happy' without it."[13] It would be a self-selective and open elite and thus, in her view, would meet the democratic test. Proposals to expand public space by including within it large economic institutions—and thereby provide ordinary men and women with an opportunity to engage in forms of political activity meaningful to themselves—were summarily rejected on the grounds that economics is not politics. More importantly, Arendt and Wolin fear that to do so would detract significantly from the general character and elevated status of the public realm.[14] In Wolin's words, it would do nothing more than to add to the "sublimation of the political."[15]

What is ironic about Arendt's and Wolin's stand is that, on the one hand, they embrace the public character of the Greek *polis* and its developmental impact on its citizens and, on the other hand, endorse for contemporary societies a "reified" Lockian conception of the public: a realm removed from the lives of the overwhelming majority of citizens and, consequently, one likely to have little, if any, developmental impact upon them.[16]

The paradox really emerges here on a double level. Participation connotes inclusion, and yet to ensure the purity of the process and to obviate the occurrence of the duplication phenomenon that formed the crux of our first paradox, theorists such as Wolin and Arendt redesign the process so that it becomes elitist and exclusionary. A paradox within a paradox emerges when one considers how the elitist theorists of participation propose to accomplish their goals. According to their view, only those individuals and groups are considered authentic participants in public decision making that do not bear immediate identifying marks linking them with one particular private interest or another. But these "authentic" individuals and groups have been nurtured in a constellation of private settings that avowedly or unwittingly inculcate a set of values, prejudices, and priorities in their inhabitants. Even if the environments in which these individuals and groups were formed strove to purify themselves from self-aggrandizement, it is doubtful that they could transcend—or even effectively counteract—the dominant climate and ideology of privatization that characterizes liberal culture. Thus—and this is the second and deeper phase of the paradox that elitist theorists of the public confront—if participation is a hopelessly contaminated process for the masses of individuals and groups within liberal society, then participation likely remains tainted even for those privileged elites that theorists such as Wolin and Arendt want to include in the participatory process.

Critics of the elitist conceptualization of the public such as Carole Pateman and Ronald Mason are intent upon expanding the concept of the public in order to provide the masses with opportunities to participate in shaping the political issues of everyday life—even issues that are trivial in comparison with Arendt's and Wolin's "common good" issues. The political is brought into being, Pateman argues, "when citizens gather together to make political decisions. Political life is thus rooted in, and forms an integral part of, social life as a whole. It is distinct from the private aspect of social life, where individuals act singularly, but it is no longer, as in liberal theory, dualistically counterposed against the private sphere of social life."[17] The major purpose of this broadly conceived definition of the political is to abolish the liberal wall of separation between politics and economics and thereby create participatory political space in areas vital to the lives of ordinary men and women. Furthermore, with the wall's collapse, rarefied equal political rights—formerly restricted to a confined area of "politics"—are transformed into potentially strong instruments for combating inequalities in power and privilege within the industrial sector.

Two seemingly opposed criticisms can be made of Pateman's conception of the political: On the one hand, it deprives society of essential private space and thus invites the dangers associated with totalitarianism, and, on the other hand, it would generate excessive fragmentation and as a consequence also endanger public space. We elaborate on each critical vantage point in turn.

One does not have to adhere to the liberal approach that conceives of participation in cost-benefit terms to appreciate the integral relationship between a realm of protected privacy and the quality of political participation. Freedom to do what one likes in private is essential to fuel and give meaning to what one does and says in public. It is this attribute of a free society that Pateman slights in her delineation of the public.[18]

To expand upon the other line of criticism, Pateman's conceptualization of full democratic participation is directed inward toward insulated groups in society. In focusing on the interrelationship of individuals within these distinct collectives, her concept of the political could well endanger the notion of the public in the sense that each collective regards the organization as "theirs," and that they, not outsiders, constitute the authoritative source of decision making.[19]

There is an unresolved tension in the choice most theorists must make between upgrading the "public" and downgrading citizen participation in discrete organizations or upgrading citizen participation in large-scale organizations and downgrading the "public." However, this tension is ignored by Pateman and others who argue that the two objectives can be complementary: that widespread participation within groups nurtures and strengthens allegiance to the public. This belief is grounded in a main premise of participatory theory: that democratic participation develops the psychological, social, and political capacities of the participants and deepens understanding of and commitment to democracy.[20] Since "widespread and effective participation," writes Mason, "is antithetical to nondemocratic forms of government, participation can only contribute to the stability and viability of democratic political processes. In this way, participation can be said to engender conditions conducive to further participation and democracy itself."[21] Benjamin Barber proclaims that participation has the "capacity of transforming dependent private individuals into free citizens and partial and private interests into public goods."[22]

Admittedly, as we have argued, participatory experience within a community may indeed transform the participant in a number of worthwhile developmental ways. But here the crucial question is whether participants will gain from their experience a capacity for a more inclusive common life beyond the interests and concerns of their particular group or community. On its face, it would seem reasonable to assume that this question could not be intelligently answered without first knowing the animating purpose that sustained a participatory community. For example, if the maximization of profits for its members were the primary aim of a particular collective, one could not reasonably expect participatory experience in this kind of environment to engender consciousness that transcends such parochial goals. Edward Greenberg's empirical study of workplace democracy is instructive in this regard. (See Chapter 6.)

The paradox of participatory theory is that within a liberal acquisitive culture participation could well lead to a greater fragmentation—to redirection of individual citizens' attention away from genuine public issues to a heightened expression of and more intense doting on private perceptions, concerns, and anxieties. However, in our view, there is a partial way out of this difficulty, which we discuss later in this chapter.

II

It was not long after the publication of *Participation and Democratic Theory* that Pateman became aware that she and other proponents of participatory democracy had not taken the feminist critique into account.[23] By failing to attack the domestic division of labor between men and women and the nonrecognition of work in the home, the theory of participatory democracy remained within the confines of patriarchal liberalism. In a series of articles she attempted to evolve a position that constitutes a genuine "alternative to the dichotomies and oppositions of patriarchal-liberalism."[24] Even though classical liberal doctrine as formulated by John Locke was directly concerned to dislodge Sir Robert Filmer's *Patriarchia* from its position of theoretical and ideological preeminence, Pateman—and feminist theorists generally—trace important continuities between patriarchal and liberal thought. The burden of their argument is "that the 'separate' liberal worlds of private and public life are actually interrelated, connected by a patriarchal structure."[25] The public world of liberal democracy presupposes the primacy of men, and this in turn is predicated upon a tacitly patriarchal familial structure in which women attend to the major household tasks, thus freeing up the men for their active public roles.

Pateman rejects three approaches pursued by feminists for coping with the implicitly patriarchal structure of liberal society. The first was advocated by John Stuart Mill in his path-breaking feminist tract *The Subjection of Women*.[26] Mill would initiate political reform at the level of the family, creating a more morally and legally egalitarian family structure. In criticizing Mill, Pateman writes that "the egalitarian family on its own, [cannot] substitute for participation in a wide variety of social institutions (especially the workplace) that Mill, in his other social and political writings, argues is the necessary education for citizenship. How can wives who have 'chosen' private life develop a public spirit? Women will thus exemplify the selfish, private beings, lacking a sense of justice, who result, according to Mill, when individuals have no experience of public life."[27]

A second approach adopted by radical feminists is to deny the dichotomy of public versus private and to claim that the family, too, is an utterly conventionally defined realm, subject to the same kinds of interventionist modifications as any institution in the public realm. A third approach embraced by some feminists is to collapse the personal into the political. A political vocabulary is as useful and illuminating in the intra-psychic and interpersonal spheres as it is in collective, social settings.

Pateman criticizes the second and third approaches because of their obliteration of the obvious reality of gender differences, which has important familial repercussions. In contrast to all three approaches, Pateman proposes a feminism that affirms "a differentiated social order within which the various dimensions are distinct but not separate or opposed, and which rests on a social conception of individuality, which includes both women and men as biologically differentiated but not unequal creatures. Nevertheless, women and men, and

the private and the public, are not necessarily in harmony." [28]
Pateman thus wants to affirm both commonality and difference between the public and the private, the masculine and
the feminine. The commonality is required so that the feminist critique will work. There are no sufficiently important in-
born distinctions between women and men to prevent women
from moving freely and authoritatively within and between
the family and public realms. There is also no acceptable
justification for men's not sharing equally in domestic tasks,
including childrearing. On the other hand, Pateman refrains
from espousing a full-fledged negation or identity thesis (the
family is all conventional claptrap; the personal is the political) because this is unjust to feminine difference. In her recent
feminist theorizing, therefore, Pateman extends her espousal
of a participationist position discussed earlier in this chapter
to encompass relations between men and women within the
family. While theoretically acknowledging the significance of
gender difference, she argues for the expansion of the concept of equality to include the variegated network of family
relations. By conceiving of the family as a pertinent setting
for the working out of persistently more and more egalitarian
relationships, Pateman has in effect theorized the family as an
additional arena of public space.

Pateman has made her case: Proponents of participatory
democracy can no longer believe that a basic democratic transformation has occurred unless patriarchal liberalism has been
overcome. We agree that a democratic revolution must include
the transcendence of patriarchal liberalism, but we disagree
that it is the function of participatory democracy to achieve this
task directly. The participatory praxis of the workplace will
likely set the stage for at least some women and men to democratically remold their attitudes and relationships at home. [29]

III

Although the liberal, neoclassical, and participationist conceptions of the public are defective, each possesses compensatory insights. The traditional liberal view underscores the importance of the private sector as a shield against state tyranny and as a resource for public vitality. However, by utilizing the concept of the public in this narrow and primarily negative fashion, the liberal view is vulnerable to the neoclassical critique that in practice it threatens the very existence of public space. The neoclassic approach, in reacting against engulfment of the public by the private, argues that the public realm ought to be reserved for dialogue focused on the good. However, in their urge to purify public space and thereby have attention focused exclusively on a transcendent public good, they have in actuality fostered the creation of a new "participatory elite." The participationists' outlook in dismissing the neoclassic view of the public as excessively narrow and elitist emphasizes the importance of expanding the public so that it will activate and nurture widespread citizen participation. Here their position, in our view, is irrefutable. However, their conception of the public is vulnerable to attack because it (1) disallows sufficient private space from government interference, and (2) it may lead, ironically, to the privatization of public space.

The dual challenge therefore confronting democratic theorists is to develop a concept of the public that incorporates the redeeming features of each of the three approaches and also to operationalize this concept so that it is able to recommend itself, at least initially, to a political culture shaped by the pursuit of self-interest.

In principle we follow John Dewey in defining the public in terms of the degree of impact a decision has upon society.[30] For Dewey, an organization or institution is a public entity if its decisions have a significant impact on a large number of people in society. We want to modify Dewey's definition by substituting community for society. Thus, as we see it, an organization or institution should be considered to be public if its decisions and nondecisions, and, indeed, its very existence, has a significant impact upon the life of the community in which it is located. The point of defining public in this way is to vitalize democratic decision making on the grassroots level and to underscore the close relationship between economic and political issues that have an impact upon the quality of community life.

This definition facilitates the realization of two primary objectives of industrial democracy. First, by stripping the legal veil of the private away from large corporations, it invites, if it does not render imperative, the democratization of these autocratically managed institutions. Second, by limiting the expansion of the public to relatively large organizations, the private sector would remain an essential haven for contemplation and experimentation free from governmental interference. For this reason private space can be seen as an invaluable resource for the cultivation of free speech. In providing a retreat from public glare and the pressures to conform to the dominant opinions of the day, it allows minorities to evolve and sharpen their position and to express it in public when they believe it is most opportune to do so.

Since, under our definition, the family is in the private sphere, are we not perpetuating patriarchal liberalism? We think not. In the first place, the notion that one's home is one's castle does not prevent the state from the enactment and vigorous enforcement of laws—such as those pertaining to marriage, divorce, and domestic violence—designed to promote greater equality between women and men. Second, although there is no direct relationship between our conception of participatory democracy (confined to an expanded though not familial public space) and patriarchal liberalism, this does not mean that participatory democracy would not have a profound indirect impact on the present subordinate status of women within the family. It is hard to believe, to repeat, that women, as well as some men, who were exposed on a regular basis to a participatory work life would not make a concerted effort to import democratic norms to spousal relations. If the major assumption of participatory theory is correct—that participatory experience generates a desire for more participation— then progress toward workplace democracy should instigate increasing struggle by women and feminist organizations for sexual equality in all areas of life, including the home.

However, the adoption of our concept of the public does not address the problems of privatization and fragmentation of the political system. For the democratizations of large corporations and the achievement of an expanded public realm taken by themselves are unlikely to resolve these defects of the political system. However, when the system itself *is energized and empowered by working-class commitment and struggle to achieve these democratic objectives,* these defects are most likely to be resolved. As is often the case in politics, the nature of the means to the goal is all-important. Here the means is class struggle, fired by the demand for participatory rights. This relationship between participatory democracy and class struggle is a crucial one that is assiduously overlooked by liberals and participationists alike. That is, they refuse to understand that a significant attraction of the theory of participatory democracy in the workplace is that working-class struggle, which is an essential means to its realization, is itself democratically productive.

To be specific, class struggle initiated from below overcomes the weaknesses of the liberal, neoclassical, and participationist positions that we have discussed. Policy outcomes, as an outgrowth of working-class protest and struggle, are invariably both public and general in their complexion in contrast to the privatized and parochial outcomes so often produced in liberal-oriented political arenas. Issues that develop, as an outgrowth of class conflict, stimulate, if we can judge from the past, the attention and concern of the best minds in public life without restricting participation, as the neoclassical writers would want, to the high-minded. Class struggle has the effect of restructuring political parties along class lines, thereby rendering them less splintered and fragmented and vulnerable to interest-group cooptation, and heightening awareness of issues that are truly national in scope.

In the next chapter we attempt to clarify the concept of democratic class struggle and its utility in a democratic polity.

Class Struggle:
A Key Concept
of Democratic Theory

8

I

In this chapter we attempt to provide a democratic justification for the idea of class struggle—showing how the legitimation of class struggle that, on the surface, appears antithetical to democratic principles is, in fact, democratic and conducive to the strengthening and growth of democracy.

We turn to James Madison's class-conflict model of politics to illuminate the current dilemmas of American democracy. Madison's model is principally contained in the tenth *Federalist* paper, which is rightly considered the best political tract ever written by an American. *The Federalist* No. 10 both highlights the underlying deficiencies of our political system at this time, as well as intimates a possible solution to them. We argue that Madison's class-conflict model, used by him as a premise in an argument intended to combat, if not totally contain, class struggle, should now be used to foster and promote such a struggle.

The tenth *Federalist*, as indeed *The Federalist* papers as a whole, are based upon three major premises. First, Madison characterizes the typical mainsprings of behavior from the perspective of Hobbesian moral psychology and thus emphasizes the centrality of the selfish and contentious desires of humans, leading potentially to a war of all against all. Madison states that even the "most frivolous and fanciful distinctions have been sufficient to kindle men's unfriendly passions and excite their most violent conflicts."[1]

Second, the conflict-prone nature of the human is exacerbated for Madison, since, again following Hobbes, he posits that our reason is instrumental to our passions. "As long as the connection subsists between his reason and his self-love," Madison writes, "[man's] opinions and his passions will have a reciprocal influence on each other; and the former will be objects to which the latter will attach themselves."[2] Third, in a prefiguration of Marxist thought, Madison argues that conflict is bound to focus "on the various and unequal distribution of property. Those who hold and those who are without property have ever formed distinct interests in society."[3]

The danger most to be avoided in a republic, therefore, is that the unpropertied masses, armed with instrumental reason and numbers, can "execute and mask its violence under the forms of the Constitution."[4] In the American republic the many have the legal power to rule, and thus the greatest harm is most likely to come from them. Madison evokes the specter of the classic economic struggle in ancient democracies between rich and poor that made those societies "spectacles of turbulence and contention."[5] The central problem for Madison thus becomes how to prevent the class struggle that results when the rich and the poor, the few and the many, confront each other in a struggle for the distribution of resources. Madison's main objective was to construct a political system that protects "the different and unequal faculties of acquiring property."[6] In retrospect, we can say that Madison's goal was to design a political system that would protect and support the burgeoning capitalist economy.

Given Madison's class orientation toward politics, it is not surprising that he rejected the historic model of the Greek *polis*, as well as Montesquieu's and Rousseau's conceptions of the small participatory state, as worthy of emulation by the nascent American republic. Instead of small states containing self-interest by fostering attachment to the common good, Madison was convinced that political participation in small societies would simply enable cliques and interests to discover and align themselves with those who shared their ambitions, resentments, and desires. "A common passion or interest will, in almost every case, be felt by a majority of the whole." When a majority is united, Madison bluntly states, "neither moral nor religious motives can be relied on as an adequate control."[7] Thus, neither civic virtue, nor religion, nor attachment to community can prevent a majority faction from arising, or enable it to be brought under control once it has been formed.

The establishment of a large republic was Madison's well-known solution to the problem of the protection of property rights. He reasoned that if in a small regime majority cohesiveness is more likely to form, then a large republic is more likely to inhibit the mutual discovery and actualization of common interest.[8] The fragmentation of interests that a large society facilitates becomes a virtue, not a vice, in Madison's republic.

The key to Madison's solution to his problem of the protection of private property is the displacement of class struggle by a struggle of fragmented interests. Class struggle represents domestic convulsion. Competition of interests, by contrast, is an emerging struggle that promotes the safety of society. As he saw it, the conflict of opposing interests would be stabilizing rather than disruptive.[9]

The deflation of conflict within a large republic was seen as not only bestowing additional benefits through a mechanism of mutual cancellation and containment of competing interests, but also by fostering a heightened role for political representation necessitated by the very enlargement of society. An extended republic, with large electoral districts, would serve "to refine and enlarge the public views, by passing them through the medium of a chosen body of citizens . . . whose wisdom may best discern the true interests of the country"[10]— that is, representatives presumably consisting of "landholders, merchants, and men of learned professions."[11] A representative system is superior to democracy (direct rule by the people), Madison bluntly stated, since it removes lawmakers from the "local prejudices" of the people.

If the masses proved unruly in one state, Madison argued, the federal structure of the country would preclude the spread of "a general conflagration through the other states."[12] Thus, "a rage for paper money, for an abolition of debts, for an equal division of property, or for any other improper or wicked project, will be less apt to pervade the whole body of the Union than a particular member of it."[13]

In the eyes of the Founding Fathers the republican principle could be reconciled with the sanctity of private property if the constitutional structure was designed first to enable "the government to control the governed, and in the next place oblige it to control itself."[14] If the influence of mass participation in political life was minimized, the first goal could be achieved. And, indeed, the pursuit of this goal has left a permanent imprint on the history of democratic politics in the United States. More than two hundred years after the founding, the fragmentation of government so ingeniously designed by the Founders remains a powerful force in minimizing mass political participation and influence in government. The second goal could be achieved by adherence to the principle of judicial review— a principle that authorizes the Supreme Court, not the people (as Jefferson proposed), to be the chief arbitrator between conflicting parties, including branches of government.

II

The Madisonian version of interest politics was, according to Samuel Huntington, "reformulated by Arthur Bentley in the early twentieth century, and it reemerged as the dominant interpretation of American politics among political scientists after World War II."[15] To be more precise, Madison's pluralist paradigm was "reformulated" and it "reemerged" by purging Madison's theory of its class base. As we have seen, "class" constitutes the dominant anxiety in Madison's thought; in pluralist theory "class" is nonexistent; groups are all. Ironically, in not perceiving the relevance of class conflict for contemporary democratic theory, democratic theorists have ignored the most promising part of Madison's argument.

Madison's version of republicanism provided the necessary protection for the private economic sphere to gain a firm foothold in society and to grow and prosper. In retrospect, however, the nation has paid a heavy price in having its political practices cast in a Madisonian mold. Madison's conceptions are still strongly reflected in our contemporary political system—a system that, on the one hand, is characterized by widespread nonparticipation and, on the other, by political egocentrism on the part of those who do participate. Both of these persistent features of the system have contributed significantly to government's inability to govern responsibly and effectively. The cultivation of a genuinely democratic political system was anathema to Madison and his colleagues. To allow ordinary men and women to gain a political voice would court the passions of the masses. The Constitution was structured, as Hannah Arendt has said, to protect private rights, not to promote public participation. It was believed that common people could best develop their capacities and personalities in the private sphere and that politics should be left to their social and intellectual betters.

The nonparticipatory legacy of the Founding Fathers has acquired strong roots in contemporary American life, especially among members of the lower socioeconomic strata. Individuals in these classes experience a sense of powerlessness and, therefore, see little relationship between their personal problems and anxieties and public issues. Consequently, members of these classes have overwhelmingly opted out of political life.

In sharp contrast to the political behavior of the lower socioeconomic strata, middle- and upper-class groups—ranging from the elderly, students, and veterans to business people and farmers—have, in increasing numbers, invaded the public realm in an effort to maximize their private benefits. Rousseau, Hegel, Marx, and Arendt would argue that the kind of political activity manifested by these middle- and upper-class groups constitutes a perversion of politics. For Madison, however, who drew no sharp distinction between selfish and enlightened interests—as long as interests dissipated or countered passions—the interest-group activities engaged in by the middle and upper classes have to be regarded as legitimate. What Madison did not anticipate was the extent to which fragmented private interests would invade and usurp public space and place in jeopardy public deliberation upon public issues. With the expansion of the electorate, the pursuit of private interests has become a form of "public greed" as a frenzied competition intensifies between interest groups for more benefits, more privileges, and, more importantly, more exemptions from law. In a real sense, democracy has been corrupted—not from the lowly ranks of the nonparticipatory masses, but from the supposed pillars and upholders of the law—the upper and middle classes.

Although it was of primary importance to Madison that the "different and unequal facilities of acquiring property" be protected, it is unlikely that he would have approved of an outcome whereby the preponderance of power within the community has shifted to the few, the privileged, and the rich.[16] Madison could not have foreseen how the protection of inequality

of ownership would spur the transformation of small entrepreneurs into robber barons and them in turn into gigantic
corporations. The diversity of ways in which power is wielded
by these corporations is incomprehensible. Even former pluralists, as we have seen, have come to the realization that these
private islands of power are not ordinary interest groups to be
treated on a par with their rivals.

It is debatable how Madison would have construed recent developments: namely, the political passivity of the lower classes,
the privatization of the legislative process, and the political
dominance of business. On the one hand, these developments
can be accommodated under a Madisonian rubric since they
are rooted in the process whereby passions are converted into
interests,[17] and, in combination, they represent an impressive
protective barrier against a mass invasion of private property.
On the other hand, however, one could argue with equal co-
gency that Madison's dread of tyranny from any quarter would
lead him to look critically upon the current imbalance of power
in American politics. Madison was fully aware that the rich,
possessing the same Hobbesian self-aggrandizing impulses as
other men, were capable of abusing power and tyrannizing
others. Although in the tenth *Federalist* he focused on the dangers of majority factions—mentioning minority factions only
twice—there is a strong basis in the logic internal to *The Federalist* No. 10 against our attributing to Madison a totally benign
attitude toward the well-to-do. The majority, in Madison's view,
would become dominant in the new republic and thus constitute the potential oppressor, while the propertied class would
represent no threat since "its sinister views" could always be
defeated by regular vote. Now, however, with the propertied
classes unrivaled in influence and power, it is possible that
Madison would recognize the need to institute compensatory
institutional mechanisms to restore a proper balance. Both we
and Madison would define the problem in the same way: how
"to secure the public good and private rights against the dan-

ger of (a dominant) faction, and at the same time to preserve the spirit and form of popular government."

Madison defined the central political problem as the threat to freedom by an overpowering majority faction. His solution was to dissipate the majority's power by institutionally transforming passion into interest and thereby inducing the fragmentation associated with interest-group politics. This remedy, however, devitalizes democracy. Today the fundamental problem of a threat to freedom remains essentially the same—except that its danger emanates from a dominant corporate minority, not from the majority. The persistence of a lopsided version of Madison's problem suggests that his class-conflict model is still applicable for addressing this problem, if the model is used, so to speak, in reverse: namely, to promote class struggle as a means to combat overbearing corporate power. Mass passivity and excessive fragmentation would also be diminished as a result of this struggle.

Madison's conception of class conflict as confrontation between rich and poor, creditors and debtors, has historically been complicated by the Marxist concept of class struggle. Our interpretation of this key concept can be best understood by contrasting it with the Marxist position.

Although Marxists often disagree among themselves concerning the nature of class (for example, whether the "Professional-Management Class" constitutes a separate and distinct class,[18] and whether nonproductive workers can be regarded as part of the working class),[19] they agree that class conflict is fundamentally a product of the relations of exploitation of production in mature capitalist societies. Exploitative relations, in turn, result from the contradiction between the socialized nature of production and the private appropriation of the means of production.

In contrast to classical Marxism, we maintain that the objective conditions that make possible (not determine) the emergence of class struggle include political and ideological as well as economic forces. This perspective allows the analyst to go beyond the overly restrictive Marxian concept of class conflict, which sees it as rooted in economic exploitation.

The worker-student revolt in France in May 1968 (during a period of economic prosperity) and more recently the broad-based mass uprising in Poland (during a period of economic depression) are examples of class conflict generated by the resentment of subordinate classes toward those in dominant positions in which political and ideological factors prevailed. In commenting on the May events in France, Michael Mann writes: " 'Surplus value,' 'class exploitation,' and even the word 'revolution' itself are notably absent from their (the workers') propaganda. Instead we find the key terms, auto-gestation, self-management and a concern to work out procedures to ensure democratic control of decision-making processes." [20] The Polish experience is also instructive in this regard. Democracy was the rallying point for workers in their revolt against autocratic rule by the Communist party and the state. Equally significant, as an outgrowth of prolonged class struggle, rank-and-file workers took democracy sufficiently seriously to protest against undemocratic decision making by their own Solidarity party leaders. Students and rank-and-file Communist party members alike demanded that democracy be adhered to by their leaders in practice as well as in theory. These revolts, together with the more recent and dramatic popular uprising against tyrannical rule in eastern Europe, underscore the overly narrow, one-dimensional view of the Marxists that "exploitative relations of production" is the cause of political upheaval.

In our view, class is a power relationship between those who dominate and those who are dominated. Thus, working men and women become a class when they "feel and articulate the identity of their [common] interests" as subordinate salary and wage workers against other men and women who occupy positions of domination over them.[21] Conceptualized in this way, a class does not exist in itself; it is the function of a relationship. Thus, unlike a group, which can be defined in terms of itself—its purposes, qualifications for membership, rules, and so on—a class can be defined only in the context of its power relationship with another class. Classes emerge therefore not prior to, but as a result of, struggle.[22]

Linking the idea of class to class struggle does not mean that struggle must be overtly manifested. If this were the case, then it would have to be conceded that the American working force is more or less classless since there is little evidence of class struggle. However, since we have conceptualized class struggle as a power relationship, and the most potent power relationship is one that is covert—in which neither the wielder of, nor the complier with, power is aware that power is being exercised (see Chapter 3), then the absence of an overt class struggle does not necessarily mean that the labor force is classless. Overt class struggle may be muted because of the dominance of the ruling class and the powerlessness of the working class. Under these conditions, the rudiments of class may emerge in the absence of overt class struggle.

Covert class struggle may be reflected in the class consciousness of working people: men and women who are aware that they are members of the working class and who resent being pushed around by those who govern their working lives. In their study *The American Perception of Class*, Vanneman and Cannon conducted a survey which showed that in 1980, 70 percent of all working Americans considered themselves working class.[23] As an example of a typical class-conscious worker, they quote Ed Sadlowski, a maverick steelworkers' union official:

> There's a certain instinct that a worker has, much more so than some candy-assed storeowner. He understands who's screwing him, but he doesn't understand how to get unscrewed. The little chamber of commerce storefront man, he never understands he's getting screwed. He's part of Main Street, America. I place

my faith in the working stiff, regardless of his hangups. He's still the most reliable guy on the street when push comes to shove.[24]

Vanneman and Cannon's study is unpersuasive, however, to the extent that their data do not reveal to what extent Sadlowski's beliefs are shared by other workers. Since he is an articulate union official, it is likely his class consciousness is more advanced than most workers. The latter may indeed be class conscious in the sense that they are aware of being members of the working class. However, some, if not the majority of these class-conscious workers, may be resigned to their fate. They may, for example, subordinate the importance of their role as workers to life after quitting time, as consumers, TV watchers, churchgoers, and the like.

Despite this flaw in their analysis, Vanneman and Cannon's book, as well as other studies in this genre, such as Sennett and Cobb's *Hidden Injuries of Class*, underscore the one-dimensionality of the value system in America, which, owing to its class dominance, prevents the emergence of a working-class ideology that could serve as an essential interpretive aid for workers to make sense of their actual experience as members of the working class. In Sadlowski's terms, workers know they have been screwed, but in the absence of a meaningful alternative ideology, they do not know how to become unscrewed.

In the next chapter we raise the issue as to whether a working-class ideology can develop in the face of a prevailing ideology that is fundamentally hostile to it. Here we want to argue that class struggle, initiated by the working class, can be an invaluable political strategy toward the democratization of an ailing pseudo-democratic polity such as exists today in the United States. Basically, there is a twofold argument for the legitimation of working-class struggle as a democratic strategy. First, in the context of American politics of the 1990s, it is the only effective means toward achieving a democratic transformation of industry. This assertion is based on the assumption that oligarchical corporate management is unwilling to co-operate in its own dismantlement, and the public is unlikely to become sufficiently aroused to demand national legislation mandating the democratization of the workplace. Second, the outgrowth of such a struggle for a democratization of indus-try, especially if the struggle is sustained over a period of time, is likely to generate a transformation of national poli-tics in which class politics become the norm—a politics in which single-issue, fragmented interests are overshadowed by national issues raised by class-oriented parties. Within the con-text of a liberal, acquisitive society, class-oriented parties, as Schattschneider (1960) and most recently Kevin Phillips (1990) have argued, are the most effective vehicle for generating citi-zen participation leading to responsive and responsible gov-ernment. From a democratic perspective, class struggle must be assessed, in other words, both in terms of its impact on the political process as well as its outcomes in industry.

Class struggle, initiated from below, is seldom regarded by most political scientists as a vital ingredient for the health of a democratic polity. On the contrary, it is usually perceived as a threat to the stability, if not to the very survival, of democracy. Political scientists often take special pride in consensual poli-tics and the institutions and procedures that "regulate" conflict and keep it safely within bounds. We dismiss this position as counterproductive to the well-being of the American politi-cal system—especially at this time when American democracy is floundering. It is a position that is based on the presump-tion that class struggle is politically destabilizing and therefore should be avoided rather than, as we have argued, that it should be encouraged when it is likely to promote democracy. We now turn to this issue by first attempting to clarify the meaning of class struggle as a democratic concept.

III

For the classical Marxist the overriding aim of class struggle is the destruction of the bourgeois state, which is seen as a precondition for the establishment of socialism. Socialism, in turn, is regarded as the precondition for the emancipation of all members of society, including the working class. For the democrat the expansion of democracy, based upon the extension of participatory rights for workers and thus the redistribution of power in favor of subordinate classes, is the goal of class struggle at this time. Each step toward the achievement of this goal is both an end in itself and a basis for further democratic advance. In the course of this struggle the aim is not to destroy the bourgeois state, but to transform it by mass political pressure from a hostile to a supportive force for greater democratization of society.

The gradual and incremental nature of this approach to class struggle, however, is regarded by the Marxist as fundamentally flawed since it affords ample time for corporate power, unions, and the state to either crush, subvert, or coopt the participatory movements involved. A democrat foresees this risk but accepts it as unavoidable. Education of workers in self-rule, acquired in the course of long and periodic struggles for the extension of democracy, is essential for the achievement of a participatory society. For a democrat, in contrast to the classical Marxist, the means by which power is realized is of paramount importance.

Under the Marxist conception of class struggle, the expectation is that class struggle will ultimately undermine itself as society approaches a classless state. This rationale for class struggle legitimates one-party rule in societies that are in the process of eradicating capitalist exploitation. However, when the inordinate power of some party elites becomes endemic to the positions they occupy in political structures, then the Marxian justification of class struggle collapses: Elite attempts

to abolish economic exploitation do not necessarily destroy—
and may, indeed, create—a new political center of domination
and thus a new exploitative class.

Even assuming the establishment of a participatory democratic society as a result of a "long revolution," one can anticipate the development of mini-class struggles between blacks
and whites, males and females, and mental and manual workers. Thus, in sharp contrast to Marxist theory, we do not envisage over the long run any one class performing in a historically
redemptive role. Heightening of class consciousness among a
continuing succession of suppressed groups, leading to class
or intraclass struggles, is required to preserve the democratic
character of society.

Leaders of democratic movements tend to solidify their
power and followers tend to become overly submissive. As
Robert Michels suggested early in the century, one of the key
functions of democracy is to combat this tendency. By promoting and legitimating class struggle and thereby fostering
widespread participation, the iron law of oligarchy would, one
hopes, be continually forestalled. A concept of class struggle
must therefore be an integral and continuing part of democratic theory.

Finally, a deep division exists between radical democrats and
Marxists concerning the correct way to decide the appropri-
ateness of class struggle as a political strategy. This issue was
the focus of an interesting exchange of views between Leon
Trotsky and John Dewey.[25] Trotsky argued that class struggle
is always justified, that "the liberating morality of the proletariat . . . deduces a rule for conduct from the laws of the
development of society, thus primarily from the class struggle,
this law of all laws." The appropriate means for working-class
liberation, in other words, follow from the dialectical laws of
history, which are institutionalized in class struggle.

Dewey rejected this position on the ground that Trotsky "deduces the correct means from the law of social development,

rather than deciding the issues on the grounds of an independent examination of measures and policies with respect to their objective consequences."[26] It could well be true, Dewey argued, that class struggle is the best means to attain the end of human liberation. But as a means, it should be justified on the basis of a critical analysis of the probable consequences of class struggle, not deduced from a supposed scientific law of history.

In line with Dewey's position, we believe that class struggle can be deemed to be democratic to the extent that its probable consequence is a stronger democracy. At this time its impact on American democracy, as we have argued, is very likely to be crucial to its well-being and growth and perhaps essential to its survival.

It might be objected that working-class struggle would only provide the ground for organizing workers to use their new-found power to dominate industries and plants for their own parochial and selfish interests. Why should it be assumed, as we have asked before, that working-class power, unlike other forms of power, would be bound to the general interest? One response to this is that workers, who were committed to the cause of workplace democracy, would be more or less bound to adhere to democratic norms of society if, for no other reason, that they would want to avoid arousing public reaction that would likely be mobilized against antidemocratic behavior. This is the overriding advantage of class politics in a democracy: Class issues would be fought out within a national arena in which the very idea of class struggle would itself be democratically contestable. Thus, for involved workers, just like for their opponents, the legitimation battle would be all-important. In the course of their struggle for the recognition of workers' participatory rights, it is likely that workers would find it strategically advantageous to transform their collective assertion "we want" into a "we are entitled to"[27]—a claim that can be justified in terms of democratic values. By acting expediently, in other words, workers would be caught up in an educative process focused on the meaning of democracy and how it applies in the real world of their own lives. Their concept of "worker participation," for example, could in the course of dialogue among themselves and outsiders be broadened to mean democratic sharing, not exclusive "worker control" of decision making in industry. In the same vein, workers might soon understand that as corporate structures become democratized, they thereby become "public" and must therefore operate in a public way. For if workers do not perceive this, they may lose the legitimation battle. Thus, in the struggle to win the day for *their* democratic demands, workers gain a deeper understanding of democracy as a doctrine dedicated to the equal concerns of all.

IV

In summary, we have argued that an analysis of Madison's tenth *Federalist* paper is useful for understanding the present in two respects. First, it sharpens our comprehension of the chronic malfunctioning of our political system. In effect, Madison's solution—fragmented interest politics and minimum citizen participation—becomes the root of our problem. Second, his invocation of a class-conflict model of politics to set the stage for his problem provides us with an important clue for resolving *our* problem, which was generated by *his* solution. To persist in ignoring Madison's approach— as though the phrase "class struggle" has been bewitched by a Marxian goblin—is to divorce democratic theory from the active concerns of a large proportion of the citizenry. Democratic theorists must explore the possibility that Madison's delineation of the problem of politics two hundred years ago offers us guidance in attempting to achieve the revitalization of democracy today.

In following Madison's lead, we contend that the adoption

of a democratic concept of class struggle could provide the crucial normative ingredient to spur a working-class movement to organize and work toward the democratization of industry. Our common bond with Madison is our commitment to the preservation of pluralism within American society. Today, however, *democratic* pluralism has the best chance to survive and grow if it is grounded in class struggle—a struggle that activates subordinate groups to organize and participate politically along class lines. Their source of power is class self-identification. And their use of this power to acquire the right to participate in all decision-making levels in the workplace is in their and the country's interest. The failure of democratic theorists to recognize this fact perpetuates the political impotence of large segments of the American population.

Democracy as Praxis

9

A tacit premise of abundance underlies the establishment and subsequent history of American constitutionalism. Such doctrines as separation of powers and checks and balances, which officially aim at inhibiting the fund of governmental power, have seemed plausible in governing a republic as vast and heterogeneous as the United States only because of the abundance of resources available for cultivation; governmental authority did not have to be immediately invoked to mitigate conflict and regulate distribution. Disadvantaged parties could strive to rectify the balance on their own by seeking out new opportunities. Also, because of the abundance of resources, when government has had to step in to regulate, it has been able to preserve a facade of neutrality. The economy was rich enough to sustain both the entrenched positions of the already powerful as well as some demands of the less powerful for an institutional stake in the game.

In the current context of diminished economic growth, the basic ground rules of American politics are in danger. The insurmountability of the budget and trade deficits is being translated into an augmented and protracted legitimation crisis. The recently created record gap between rich and poor in this country is continuing to widen. Recent national administrations have been unable or unwilling to check falling wages— thus leaving most American workers worse off then they were twenty years ago—or to reduce the trade imbalance, which erodes the standard of living for wage earners generally. As for the quality of life of the least-well-off members of American society: The collective efforts of all layers of government in the United States have been unable to decrease the crime rate—which is the highest of any industrial nation, alleviate the plight of the homeless, curb an unparalleled drug problem, or restore public schools so that they function as educational institutions.

The inability of our governments to govern stems largely from the irrational division of responsibility and power among federal, state, and local governments, on the one hand, and from the archaic division and checks instituted between the executive and legislative branches of the federal government, on the other. In epochs of abundance governmental irresponsibilities were usually papered over by money. In a period of declining economic growth and perpetually unbalanced budgets the incapacity of government to govern responsibly becomes exposed. When government does act in this climate, it can often no longer mask its class bias. Most Americans must be struck by the paradox that a government willing to commit billions of taxpayer dollars to bail out the savings and loans institutions and then to go to war, at a cost of a billion dollars a day, continues to cut back entitlement programs for social needs.

A vacuum of political leadership and inventiveness on the domestic front has deepened the crisis. The zero-sum economic context in which we all appear to be living has led to a period of governmental paralysis in which we lack any political vision to direct us out of our difficulties. The right relies on privatization as a panacea for our economic problems, but privatization intensifies the gap between rich and poor in American society. The left seems ideologically bankrupt, unable to transcend worn-out Keynesian and welfare-state policies.

The economic and political conditions we have been describing bear a disturbing resemblance to the textbook case associated with the rise of fascism. However, when viewed from a more optimistic perspective, they can also be seen as conditions favorable to the promotion of structural democratic reform. As Kevin Phillips argues, they are congenial to the growth of class politics and the ascendancy of the Democratic party. If this were to occur, the nature and eventual outcome of social reform would have to be shaped—in contrast to past reforms—under the constraints of diminished public and private resources. The overwhelming public and private debt provides favorable conditions for the adoption of basic reforms for two reasons. First, it would discourage the left from supporting costly welfare-state programs. Instead, the left would be pressed to fight for structural reforms that do not require large financial outlays. In light of its growing favor among social scientists, workplace democracy could well become its leading proposal. Second, heavily indebted corporations would be seriously handicapped in their capacity to kill, deflect, or coopt a proposal that was fundamentally against their interest, such as a plan to democratize corporate structures. However, in the absence of a strong labor movement committed to fight for such a reform, workers would be unlikely to exploit corporate vulnerability. It could well be a case, as observed by Gramsci, in which they would remain in the hegemonic grip of the ruling class and be unable to recognize—much less take advantage of—the inability of the ruling elite to govern. What is needed consequently is an "appropriate political initiative [to] liberate the economic thrust from the dead weight of traditional politics."[1]

The first essential step toward fostering an initiative of this

kind is to reject the assumption underlying the "false consciousness" argument of the classic Marxists. It holds that subordinate classes internalize the norms, values, and beliefs of
the dominant class so that they see their failures and powerlessness as justified. Although the Marxist assumption has
been shown empirically to be partially true,[2] it is mislead-
ing, ignoring the evidence that workers tend to be politically
schizophrenic, holding to dominant values and thus accepting
their lot, while at the same time subscribing to deviant values,
expressed in class terms.[3] To adopt David Garson's phrase,
American workers are essentially "multi-conscious," holding
to inconsistent and contradictory beliefs.[4] Most workers he
interviewed, for example, considered themselves to be conservative or moderate politically, while agreeing to the statement that "American needs a new political party built around
the interests of working people." While a large majority re-
sponded affirmatively to the statement that "the laws favor
the rich," an almost equally large majority rejected the elitist for the pluralist model in describing the political process.[5]
Although workers' beliefs tend to be filled with inconsistencies
and contradictions, this tendency becomes less so when they
express their values in concrete terms that relate to everyday
reality. Then they indicate their adherence largely to deviant
values. However, despite holding to these values, American
workers remain politically complacent, it can be argued, not
only because of their "multi-consciousness"—a mix of deviant
and dominant-oriented values—but because of their lack of a
philosophy unifying the values that result from their concrete
experiences with their vague populist notions. Their values are
fractured, and hence they feel powerless to change their situation. It is not that the working class has been locked into and
manipulated by a cultural hegemony. It is rather that a liberal
democratic polity perpetuates "values that do not aid the working class to interpret the reality it actually experiences."[6] In
the absence of an alternative philosophy that enables workers

to judge their situation and promotes the adoption of a militant course of action, the working class remains immobilized. When "disaffection is not energized by any meaningful vision of an alternative mode of work, organization, or ownership," worker complacency is the rule.[7]

This argument suggests that militancy and radicalism can be nurtured and developed within the existing hegemonic order. Since workers are not locked into an ideological monolith—they do have deviant values, albeit inconsistent—we need not repeat the mistake of deferring social change until we inculcate "socialist consciousness" within the working class.

What is required at this juncture is an alternative vision which effectively connects the concrete concerns, needs, and anxieties of working-class people with what they would consider to be their democratic right to share equally, as individuals, in decision making on all levels of the enterprises in which they work. Their right to participate in the workplace should be formulated as one of their essential political rights—a right worth struggling for both for their own and the nation's well-being. This concept of the right of participation should be broadly conceived as something that all democratic citizens have in common, whether as residents of communities or as workers locked into business, professional, or governmental bureaucracies. Conceived in this way, democracy could again become an ideology of the people—an ideology that would not only stir workers to struggle for their rights but would also provide, in the course of that struggle, an ideal basis upon which to build a majority coalition, including community and neighborhood organizations, as well as other groups such as minorities, women's-rights groups, and the unemployed who have equally legitimate claims to this right.

A strategy of this kind, which focuses on the struggle of workers to secure their participatory rights, has merit on several grounds. First, within the context of the rich history of mass struggle in America, it can be seen as a strategy that has a chance of success. Mass protest in the past has been especially effective when it has been linked to democracy. A recurring reason for the protests has been that the hegemonically prevailing forces could not or would not fulfill their promises. Almost without exception, American participants in mass protest—whether the struggle was waged on the western frontier or in southern towns, factories or black ghettoes—perceived their grievances as manifesting a denial of the principles of equality and freedom rooted in the traditional idea of American democracy.[8] And each of these struggles, whether it advanced the right to vote, freedom from servitude, or freedom from ethnic, racial, or sexual discrimination, was provoked by the political system's failure to live up to its democratic commitments. Moreover, as socioeconomic and political conditions changed, the concepts of equality and freedom that were adopted inevitably expanded into new interpretations that were applicable to democratic claimants. Diverse groups have claimed and fought for new and expanded rights, such as protection from occupational hazards or toxic wastes, the availability of adequate health care, and the right of privacy as reasonable extensions of rights firmly embodied in democratic thought. Significantly, rights from this list that have been accepted, either formally or tacitly, reflect an expanding concept of democracy, an expansion, as Samuel Bowles and Herbert Gintis argue, that has charted a transformation from property to human rights.[9] All of these claims, both those accepted and those rejected (the latter includes the right to welfare and the right to work), have one important characteristic in common: Their proponents considered them eminently justifiable and legitimate in terms of American democracy. Democracy served as a moral impetus for achieving a greater degree of equality and freedom. Furthermore, the idea of democracy can continue to function as a creatively disruptive force in the polity, especially in provoking protest and struggle against the contradiction between oligarchical rule in the workplace and the idea of democracy.

A second merit of a strategy focused on worker participatory rights is that it can be supported on economic as well as political and moral grounds. For, as we have seen in Chapter 5, increased productivity and efficiency in the new complex, technologically oriented enterprise calls for the replacement of rigid hierarchies by flexible, decentralized modes of decision making, with participation by professionals, technicians, and workers on all levels of the operation. Workplace democracy, in short, makes good economic sense. Thus it serves either as a present or a future thorn in the side of management: It cannot be removed without incurring a loss in productivity and efficiency, and management cannot promote its growth without undermining the legitimacy of oligarchical control of the enterprise.

Third, the strategy can be closely linked to a major anxiety, if not trauma, that many workers have suffered in recent years, namely, job insecurity. A primary source of this insecurity is plant closings. "The specter of plant shutdowns," writes Christopher Gunn, "has left workers and whole communities feeling increasingly threatened over the past decade. . . . Workers and community leaders share a desire not to be caught again by a decision made in some distant corporate headquarters that will cut off a part of their lifeblood. . . . The threat of economic dislocation has started many working Americans imagining a different way of running their industries and organizing their work." [10]

Plant closings have also had a shattering impact on organized labor. Collective bargaining has traditionally held to the tacit presupposition that the plants and the workers were constants and that the only items subject to negotiation were the terms of employment. The basic assumption was that capital would continue to invest in its domestic enterprises. Now, however, with the flight of capital abroad, the entire fabric of collective bargaining is in jeopardy. Accordingly, the alternative of worker participation in corporate investment decisions undoubtedly has taken on a new and profound significance in the minds of labor leaders.[11] The alternative vision we are proposing here would appeal to union leaders and rank and file determined to build a labor movement that is once again a major force in shaping public policy.

The strategy focusing on participatory rights has also become relevant to professional and technical workers—including school teachers, university professors, doctors, and scientists—as economic growth diminishes and the intensity of competition in the global economy increases. Despite the technological rationale for expanding the decision-making power of this group of workers as a way to increase productivity, there is countervailing pressure in a time of financial constraint to "proletarianize" them. As governmental, university, and corporate budgets become more restrictive, scientists' discretion to determine the nature of their research and how their work will be used declines, class size and teaching load of college instructors go up along with increased pressure to publish, engineers are subject to increased productivity schedules, and social workers are required to take higher case loads and are forced to act like policemen.[12] Arbitrary decisions by administrators become especially apparent and galling to professional workers in a period of financial exigency. As professors, for example, our customary indifference toward budgetary matters of the university has abruptly disappeared in the recent lean years when we became quite aware that each dollar spent by the administration on the promotion of the football team and the expansion of the administrative staff was a dollar withheld from improving the quality of teaching and research. Our academic colleagues are slowly beginning to realize that governance of the university must be democratized if its primary objectives as an educational institution are to be preserved and advanced.

In the fourth place, a strategy that underscores the need to expand participatory rights can be used effectively to build a mass movement bridging working and middle-class groups, including environmental, neighborhood, civil rights, and women's organizations. Admittedly, at this time there is a wide breach between postindustrial, middle-class participatory groups and the working class. The separation and hostility between them, however, are ameliorable. For although currently undercultivated, a common interest can be forged between the two coalitions. This interest can be expressed both negatively and positively: negatively, by a shared position of subordination in the world; positively, by a shared latent or overt interest in acquiring meaningful participation in the determination of policy that affects them and their communities. Common action based upon this mutual interest depends upon the development of an awareness that each class is politically dependent upon the other: Without the political support of the working class, the quality-of-life concerns of the middle class are less likely to be acknowledged and resolved adequately; and without the contribution of the radical thought of middle-class intellectuals, working-class groups will be less likely to mount a meaningful demand for worker participation in industry.

Just as in the civil rights movement of the 1950s and 1960s middle-class intellectuals joined with African American activists to spearhead protest against racial discrimination, so, too, in an emerging worker-participation movement a comparable alliance between classes makes sense. Middle-class intellectuals who are propelled, for example, by environmental issues might see the connection between greater worker participation in workplace decision making and greater equalization of power in society generally as a means of achieving their demands in the environmental area. Thus, they may help lift the locally rooted grievances of trade unions out of their traditional collective-bargaining setting and encourage them to build a labor movement committed to a political struggle to achieve economic democracy. The link with the working class, contributing insight and militancy derived from the everyday experience of workers, could in turn nurture new and fresh ideas and engender new coalitions among intellectuals.

In sum, a strategy focusing on the expansion of participatory rights appears to us as the most effective way to translate democratic theory into action—action in the form of political mobilization by the labor movement and its allies committed to struggle toward the realization of workplace democracy.

In our view, however, some advocates of participatory democracy, such as Bowles and Gintis as well as Heckscher have overemphasized the social significance of the recent advance in the agenda of rights.[13] These newly won rights are indeed important, but this advance does not appear to justify the optimistic assessment "that a democratic and egalitarian society might come about through the continuing expansion of citizen rights to new arenas of society, notably the economy, through the creation of new forms of collective rights, and through the limitation of property rights."[14]

The recent expansion of employee rights has affected comparatively few workers, since it comprises mainly rights protecting women, minorities, handicapped, homosexuals, and others against discrimination in the workplace. Neither Bowles and Gintis nor Hecksher mention that during this same period the National Labor Relations Board has withdrawn from being a staunch and aggressive defender of labor's rights into an agency that tolerates employers' gross violation of the Wagner Act. At the same time, Occupational Safety and Health Administration (OSHA) underwent a radical change from being a rigorous protector of workers against workplace hazards to an agency renowned for its laxity and timidity. These drastic diminutions in performance of the two government agencies that most affect the well-being of American workers confront proponents of economic democracy with a cruel irony: While a comparatively few workers benefit from what Bowles and Gintis described as a "continuing expansion of citizen rights to new arenas of society," basic rights against arbitrary dismissal and health and safety hazards in the workplace, once enjoyed by a large number of workers, are now in jeopardy. On balance, these conflicting trends in worker rights have amounted to a decline in the net freedom and security of American workers. This assessment is strengthened when these trends are seen within the context of the existing power imbalance between capital and labor. Trade unions have lost power to the point where they now seem easy victims of the strategy of an increasing number of companies to hire strike breakers as permanent employees in an attempt to destroy unions.

Heckscher's and Bowles and Gintis's positions fail to distinguish between *protective* and *participatory* rights. Protective rights are negative, in the sense that they ensure workers' freedom from a proscribed arbitrary act. Participatory rights are positive, since they enable workers to express and exercise their own judgment in a collective process of decision making. This difference reflects a deeper difference between the two: Unlike protective rights, which guarantee the conditions of freedom, participatory rights, when exercised, are transformed into acts of freedom themselves. As assertions of freedom, they are self-generative and thus foster a desire by participants for more participation, more responsibility, and more power.

As is evident throughout our essay, we recognize the role of dialectical forces in the expansion of rights, including participatory rights, in the economy and in the concept of democracy itself. Because of the qualitative hiatus between protective and participatory rights, however, we suspect that dialectical factors left to themselves have limits, the most important of which may be their inability to produce economic democracy.

The difference between protective and participatory rights is reflected in the difference between the welfare state, and its role in the protection and implementation of rights, and a participatory society, which has begun in a limited way to recognize and protect participatory rights. In the welfare state individuals receive from the state a variety of services, goods, and protections in accordance with their rights to be free from a range of abuses and insecurities, including hunger, homelessness, unemployment, and discrimination based on race, gender, and sexual preference. Although the state's role in securing these rights is essential to a free people, the state's intervention is not without its cost in terms of freedom. For as the state expands its bureaucratic funding, services, and supervision of rights, it deepens the dependency of the people on the state. Once each group gains the recognition of its claimed right by the state, it tends to become politically passive; at best, it adopts a politically defensive posture, focused on the protection of its right. With regard to participatory rights, the state will probably also serve, at least initially, as a protector of those limited rights that have been recognized. Here the dependency factor is substantially less, with no reliance on the state for either funding or services. The basic difference, however, is that participation cannot be delegated and it cannot be institutionalized. It can only be personally undertaken—and enacted and reenacted. The sense of empowerment that it affords suggests that it is contagious both for the person herself or himself and for others placed in comparable environments.

Bowles and Gintis and Heckscher assume that the expansion of rights, qua rights, will gradually erode property rights—owing primarily to contradictions within the politico-economic system—and thus that one can be reasonably assured that the dialectical process will produce economic democracy. By rely-

ing on a supposedly irresistible trend toward the expansion
of rights, they argue in effect that the advocates of economic
democracy need not be concerned by such matters as the transformation of the concept of the corporation from a private to
a public entity, the legitimation of class struggle as a democratic concept, and the educative value for workers of a long
collective participatory struggle to secure participatory rights
in the workplace. They miss the point that the expansion of
protective rights by itself contributes little, if anything, to the
dismantling of the corporate hierarchy and its replacement
by a democratic mode of decision making. The autonomy of
management to make the crucial decisions on the magnitude
and type of investments, composition of the labor force, location of plants, and so forth, is threatened only by workers'
participatory rights, which enable workers to exercise power,
and not by protective rights. Because of this difference, capital is considerably less resistant to granting workers protective
rights than it is to according them participatory rights. Under
certain conditions management may indeed be receptive to
granting protective rights to separate and discrete groups of
workers, since it may foster discord and division among members of the workforce. From management's point of view, there
is a fundamental difference between being confronted by a
discrete group of workers demanding recognition of a protective right and its being confronted by all the workers, united
behind an egalitarian demand for recognition of participatory rights. To accede to the latter demand, even if limited
to the shop floor, would be to set a precedent, grounded on
the sanctity of participatory democratic rights. Management
would then be vulnerable to the obvious challenge: If democratic decision making is the right and appropriate process
for the shop floor, why not for other levels of the company?
Clearly, the demand from below for the recognition of this
basic right will be fiercely resisted by capital. But this should
not deter advocates of economic democracy from focusing on

this right and assigning it primary importance. By establishing the democratic frontier at protective rights and not forging beyond them toward an agenda of participatory rights, we might be withdrawing from what at this juncture in American history is democratically attainable—and thus defaulting on the promise of democracy. We must heed the dictum of Max Weber "that man would not have attained the possible unless time and again he had reached out for the impossible." The time to commit ourselves intellectually, morally, and politically to the realization of participatory rights is now.

Notes

Chapter 1

1. E. E. Schattschneider, *The Semi-Sovereign People: A Realist's View of Democracy in America* (New York: Holt, Rinehart and Winston, 1960), p. 141.

2. Charles Lindblom, *Politics and Markets: The World's Political Economic Systems* (New York: Basic Books, 1977).

3. Ibid., p. 188.

4. *New York Times*, Oct. 15, 1990, p. B 9.

5. Kevin Phillips, *Politics of Rich and Poor* (New York: Random House, 1990), p. 24.

6. Ibid., p. 15. Also see Tom Wicker, "The Holes in the Economy," *New York Times*, Sept. 2, 1988.

7. Phillips, *Politics of Rich and Poor*, p. XI. Data on distribution of wealth, as distinguished from income, reflects a most inegalitarian profile among American classes. A study sponsored by the U.S. Congress revealed that in 1983 the top 0.5 percent of all households owned more than 45 percent of the nation's privately held net wealth, excluding equity in personal residences. The top 1 percent of the nation's households owned about 53 percent of all income-producing wealth; and the top 10 percent owned 83 percent of it. The bottom nine-tenths of the nation's families owned the rest—less than 17 percent of net private wealth. See R. B. DuBoff, "Long-Term Economic Growth: Trends, Triumphs, Paradoxes" (unpublished manuscript, 1988), p. 11. Also see Stephen J. Rose, *The American Profile Poster: Who Owns What* (New York: Pantheon, 1986), p. 31; and *New York Times*, Sept. 23, 1986. Between the late 1940s and 1983 the distribution of wealth in the United States became more unequal, with the share held by the top one-half of 1 percent of the population rising, espe-

cially after the early 1970s (DuBoff, "Long-Term Economic Growth," p. 11).

8. Thomas Edsall, *The New Politics of Inequality* (New York: W. W. Norton, 1984), p. 210.

9. Charles Heckscher, *The New Unionism: Employee Involvement in the Changing Corporation* (New York: Basic Books, 1988), p. 4.

10. *New York Times*, Sept. 3, 1990, p. A20.

11. Charles Lindblom, "Another State of Mind: APSA Presidential Address," *American Political Science Review* 76 (March 1982): 9.

12. Phillips, *Politics of Rich and Poor*.

13. Adam Przeworski, *Capitalism and Social Democracy* (New York: Cambridge University Press, 1985), pp. 138–65; Claus Offe, *Contradictions of the Welfare State* (Cambridge, Mass.: MIT Press, 1984), pp. 243–50; and James O'Connor, *The Fiscal Crisis of the State* (New York: St. Martin's Press, 1973).

14. See Ida Susser, *Norman Street: Poverty and Politics in an Urban Neighborhood* (New York: Oxford University Press, 1982); and Irving Howe, ed., *Beyond the Welfare State* (New York: Schocken Books, 1982).

15. Carole Pateman, *Participation and Democratic Theory* (Cambridge: Cambridge University Press, 1970).

16. Peter Bachrach, "Participation and Democratic Theory," in J. Roland Pennock and John Chapman, eds., *Participation in Politics* (New York: Lieber-Atherton Press, 1975).

17. Samuel Bowles and Herbert Gintis, *Democracy and Capitalism: Property, Community, and the Contradictions of Social Thought* (New York: Basic Books, 1986), p. 125.

18. Walter Dean Burnham, "Why Americans Don't Vote," *New Republic*, May 9, 1988, p. 31.

19. Amy Gutmann, *Liberal Equality* (New York: Cambridge University Press, 1980), p. 181.

20. We need, in the words of Fred Dallmayr (summarizing the thought of Michel Foucault paraphrasing ideas of Gilles Deleuze), to consider "the possibility of a new or 'post-modern' kind of pluralism deviating from both liberal and pre-liberal models of democracy—a pluralism which is predicated neither on status or other ascriptive factors nor on . . . utilitarian interests, and which may be called a 'practical-ontological' type since it relies on concrete life experiences or practical modes of life." Fred R. Dallmayr, "Democracy and Post-Modernism," *Human Studies* 10 (1986): 163.

21. Schattschneider, *The Semi-Sovereign People*, p. 71.

22. Quoted in James S. Coleman, *Community Conflict* (New York: Macmillan, 1957), p. 17.

Chapter 2

1. George Kateb, "The Moral Distinctiveness of Representative Democracy," *Ethics* 91 (1981): 357.

2. Hanna Pitkin, *Representation* (New York: Atherton Press, 1969), p. 5.

3. C. B. Macpherson, *Democratic Theory* (London: Oxford University Press, 1973), p. 51.

4. John Dunn, "Democracy Unretrieved, or the Political Theory of Professor Macpherson," *British Journal of Political Science* 4 (1974): 489–500.

5. Steven Lukes, "The Real and Ideal World of Democracy," in Alkis Kantos, ed., *Power, Possessions and Freedom* (Toronto: University of Toronto Press, 1979), p. 15.

6. Herbert McCloskey, "Consensus and Ideology in American Politics," *American Political Science Review* 58 (1987): 258–82; Seymour Martin Lipset, *Political Man* (Garden City, N.Y.: Doubleday, 1963).

7. Thomas Dye and Harmon Zeigler, *The Irony of Democracy* (Pacific Grove, Calif.: Brooks/Cole, 1987); Samuel Huntington, "United States," in Michael Crozier et al., eds., *Crisis of Democracy* (New York: New York University Press, 1976).

8. Peter Bachrach, *The Theory of Democratic Elitism* (Boston: Little, Brown, 1967).

9. Dye and Zeigler, *Irony of Democracy*, p. 3.

10. Ibid., p. 446.

11. Quoted in Jack Nagel, *Participation* (Englewood, N.J.: Prentice Hall, 1987), p. 65.

12. Ibid., p. 58.

13. Ibid., p. 59.

14. Amy Gutmann, *Liberal Equality* (New York: Cambridge University Press, 1980), p. 94.

15. Sidney Verba and Norman Nie, *Participation in America: Political Democracy and Social Equality* (New York: Harper & Row, 1972), p. 277.

16. Gutmann, *Liberal Equality*, p. 196.

17. Jennifer Hochschild, *The New American Dilemma* (New Haven, Conn.: Yale University Press, 1984), p. 102.

18. J. Roland Pennock, *Democratic Theory* (Princeton, N.J.: Princeton University Press, 1982), pp. 459–60.

19. F. M. Barnard and R. A. Vernon, "Pluralism, Participation, and Politics," *Politics and Society* 3 (1975): 185.

20. Ibid., p. 185.

21. Kateb, "Moral Distinctiveness of Representative Democracy," p. 372.

22. Ibid., p. 373.

23. Robert Dahl, *Who Governs? Democracy and Power in an American City* (New Haven, Conn.: Yale University Press, 1961).

24. Nagel, *Participation*, p. 66.

25. Pennock, *Democratic Theory*, pp. 210–35.

26. Kateb, "Moral Distinctiveness of Representative Democracy," p. 359.

27. Ibid., p. 373.

28. Dahl, *Who Governs?* pp. 89–103.

29. Huntington, "United States," pp. 113–15.

30. Ibid., p. 114.

31. Dye and Zeigler, *Irony of Democracy*, p. 448.

32. Ibid., p. 448.

33. Gutmann, *Liberal Equality*, p. 190.

34. Carole Pateman, "Sublimation and Reification: Locke, Wolin, and the Liberal Democratic Conception of the Political," *Politics and Society* 5 (1975): 444.

35. Stephen Borstein and Sapsin K. Fine, "Workers' Participation and Self Government in France," paper delivered at the Annual Meeting of the American Political Science Association, 1976.

36. Robert Dahl, *A Preface to Economic Democracy* (Berkeley: University of California Press, 1985), p. 123.

37. Edward Greenberg, "Industrial Self-Management and Political Attitudes," *American Political Science Review* 75 (1981): 29–42.

38. Dahl, *Preface to Economic Democracy*, p. 124.

39. *Economist*, Oct. 31, 1981, p. 84, quoted in ibid., p. 124.

40. Edward Greenberg, *Workplace Democracy: The Political Effects of Participation* (Ithaca, N.Y.: Cornell University Press, 1986), p. 103.

41. Dahl, *Preface to Economic Democracy*, p. 123.

42. Nagel, *Participation*, p. 61.

43. John Schaar, "Legitimacy in the Modern State," in Phillip Green and Sanford Levinson, eds., *Power and Community* (New York: Pantheon Books, 1970), p. 313.

44. Lao Tzu, *The Way of Life* (New York: Perigee Books, 1980), p. 34.

45. Antonio Gramsci, *Selections from the Prison Notebooks* (New York: International, 1971). Gramsci's underscoring of the need to continually democratize leadership strata in a participatory movement—to foster an unending dialectic of hegemony counter hegemony—finds a significant resonance in the thought of Michel Foucault. Foucault argues that "the measure of the plebs is not so much what stands outside relations of power as rather what functions as their limit, their underside, their counter-stroke, that which responds to every advance of power by a movement of disengagement. Hence it forms the motivation for every new development of networks of power." Michel Foucault, *Power/Knowledge*, ed. Colin Gordon (New York: Pantheon Books, 1980), pp. 136, 138. Cited in Fred Dallmayr, "Democracy and Post-Modernism," *Human Studies* 10 (1986): 165. Foucault thus suggests a theorizing of participation as disengagement, as the countermove to power—and therefore also as the initiating moment in the formation of new networks of power. The continual sensitizing to new emergences of power propels new social strata—and hence new individuals—to aspire to positions of power.

46. Benjamin Barber, "Command Performance," *Harper's Magazine* 250 (April 1975): 51–54.

47. James Burns, *Leadership* (New York: Harper & Row, 1978).

48. Our interpretation of the role played by class struggle in inducing governmental authorities during the New Deal period to pass legislation—such as the Wagner Act—that enhanced workers' power is a subject of continuing controversy in the scholarly literature. The state autonomist view as espoused by Theda Skocpol and Kenneth Finegold, for example, argues that "shifts in electoral politics, not increases in workplace militancy, were . . . what heightened 'labor influence' on legislation—and liberal influence more generally—between 1934 and 1935." Theda Skocpol and Kenneth Finegold, "Explaining New Deal Labor Policy," *American Political Science Review* 84 (1990):

1300. We, however, find more persuasive the riposte of their disputant in the same journal's "Controversy," Michael Goldfield, when he says that "the results of the 1934 election are inexplicable without direct causal reference to the social protest environment." *American Political Science Review*, p. 1306.

49. See Frances Fox Piven and Richard Cloward, *Regulating the Poor: The Functions of Public Welfare* (New York: Pantheon Books, 1971).

Chapter 3

1. For an excellent analysis of the problem of contestability, see William Connolly, *The Terms of Political Discourse* (Princeton, N.J.: Princeton University Press, 1983), pp. 10–44.

2. Robert Dahl, "Concept of Power," *Behavioral Science* 2 (1957): 202.

3. Nelson W. Polsby, *Community Power and Political Theory* (New Haven, Conn.: Yale University Press, 1963), pp. 3–4.

4. Michael Parenti, "Power and Pluralism: A View from Below," *Journal of Politics* 32 (1970): 501–29.

5. Peter Bachrach and Morton S. Baratz, *Power and Poverty: Theory and Practice* (New York: Oxford University Press, 1970), p. 44.

6. Ibid., p. 50.

7. Robert Dahl, *Who Governs? Democracy and Power in an American City* (New Haven, Conn.: Yale University Press, 1961), p. 92.

8. Steven Lukes, *Power: A Radical View* (London: Macmillan Press, 1974), p. 23.

9. Ibid., p. 34. Also see Connolly, *The Terms of Political Discourse*, pp. 88 and 102.

10. Connolly, *The Terms of Political Discourse*, p. 106.

11. John Gaventa, *Power and Powerlessness: Quiescence and Rebellion in an Appalachian Valley* (Oxford: Oxford University Press, 1980).

12. William Connolly, "On 'Interests' in Politics," *Politics and Society* 2 (1972): 64.

13. See Grenville Wall, "The Concept of Interest in Politics," *Politics and Society* 5 (1975): 487–510; Ted Benton, "Realism, Power and Objective Interests," in Keith Graham, ed., *Contemporary Political Philosophy* (New York: Cambridge University Press, 1982); and Isaac Balbus, "The Concept of Interest in Politics," *Politics and Society* 1 (1971): 487–510.

14. Sidney Verba and Norman Nie, *Participation in America: Political Democracy and Social Equality* (New York: Harper & Row, 1972), p. 2.

15. This is a modification of Jack Nagel's conception of participation. Jack Nagel, *Participation* (Englewood Cliffs, N.J.: Prentice-Hall, 1987), p. 1.

16. Ronald Mason, *Participatory and Workplace Democracy: A Theoretical Development in Critique of Liberalism* (Carbondale: Southern Illinois University Press, 1982), p. 13.

17. Ibid., p. 20.

18. Donald W. Keim, "Participation in Contemporary Democratic Theories," in J. Roland Pennock and John W. Chapman, eds., *Participation in Politics* (New York: Lieber-Atherton, 1975).

19. Samuel Bowles and Herbert Gintis, *Democracy and Capitalism: Property, Community, and the Contradictions of Social Thought* (New York: Basic Books, 1986), p. 118.

20. Bachrach and Baratz, *Power and Poverty*, p. 43.

21. E. E. Schattschneider, *The Semi-Sovereign People: A Realist's View of Democracy in America* (New York: Holt, Rinehart and Winston, 1960), p. 71.

22. Richard Miller, *Analyzing Marx: Morality, Power, and History* (Princeton, N.J.: Princeton University Press, 1984), pp. 142–67.

23. Nicos Poulantzas, a leading neo-Marxist, defined power as "the capacity of a social class to realize its specific objective interests." *Political Power and Social Classes* (London: N.L.B. and Sheed & Ward, 1973), p. 71.

24. Antonio Gramsci, *Selections from the Prison Notebooks* (New York: International, 1971), pp. 210–11.

25. Sudipta Kaviraj, "Determination" (unpublished paper, New Delhi, 1989), p. 24.

26. Ibid., p. 25.

27. John Kenneth Galbraith, *The New Industrial State*, 3d ed. (Boston: Houghton, Mifflin, 1976), p. 176.

28. Jon Elster, "Sour Grapes—Utilitarianism and the Genesis of Wants," in Amartya Sen and Bernard Williams, eds., *Utilitarianism and Beyond* (Cambridge: Cambridge University Press, 1983), p. 227.

29. Fred Block, "The Ruling Class Does Not Rule," *Socialist Revolution* 7, no. 3 (1977): 6–28. Also see Martin Carnoy, *The State and Political Theory* (Princeton, N.J.: Princeton University Press, 1984).

30. Block, "The Ruling Class," p. 15.

31. See Adam Przeworski, *Capitalism and Social Democracy* (New York: Cambridge University Press, 1985), p. 138.

32. Charles Lindblom, *Politics and Markets: The World's Political Economic Systems* (New York: Basic Books, 1977), p. 17.

33. Claus Offe, *Disorganized Capitalism*, ed. John Keane (Cambridge, Mass.: MIT Press, 1985), pp. 185–86.

34. Ibid., p. 250.

35. Paul Peterson, *City Limits* (Chicago: University of Chicago Press, 1981), p. 210.

36. Clarence Stone, "Systemic Power in Community Decision Making," *American Political Science Review* 74 (Dec. 1980): 985.

37. See Clarence Stone, *Economic Growth and Neighborhood Discontent* (Chapel Hill: University of North Carolina Press, 1976), and Edward Hayes, *Power Structure and Urban Policy* (New York: McGraw-Hill, 1972).

38. Peterson, *City Limits*, p. 119.

39. Polsby, *Community Power and Political Theory*, p. 118.

40. See Grant McConnell, *Private Power and American Democracy* (New York: Alfred A. Knopf, 1967); and Przeworski, *Capitalism and Social Democracy*, p. 138.

41. Lindblom, *Politics and Markets*, pp. 246–47.

42. See Madison, No. 10 of Alexander Hamilton, John Jay, and James Madison, *The Federalist: A Commentary on the Constitution of the United States, Being a Collection of Essays Written in Support of the Constitution Agreed upon September 17, 1787 by the Federal Convention from the Original Text of Alexander Hamilton, John Jay and James Madison*, with an introduction by Edward Mead Earle (New York: Modern Library, 1941).

43. Nagel, *Participation*, p. 58.

44. Schattschneider, *Semi-Sovereign People*, p. 31.

45. Verba and Nie, *Participation in America*, p. 335.

46. Ibid., p. 342.

47. Quoted in Stone, "Systemic Power in Community Decision Making," p. 983.

48. Michael Parenti, "Power and Pluralism: A View from Below," *Journal of Politics* 32 (1970): 501–29.

49. Nagel, *Participation*, p. 5.

Chapter 4

1. Alfred Diamant, "Industrial Democracy in Western Europe," paper delivered at the Annual Meeting of the American Political Science Association, 1982. Also see Edward Greenberg, *Workplace Democracy: The Political Effects of Participation* (Ithaca, N.Y.: Cornell University Press, 1986); and Carmen Sirianni, ed., *Worker Participation and the Politics of Reform* (Philadelphia: Temple University Press, 1987).

2. Hannah Arendt, *On Revolution* (New York: Viking Press, 1963).

3. Antonio Gramsci, "Soviets in Italy," *New Left Review*, Sept.–Oct. 1968.

4. Andre Gorz, "Workers' Control Is More Than Just That," in Jerry Hunnius et al., eds., *Workers' Control* (New York: Vintage Books, 1973).

5. Diamant, "Industrial Democracy in Western Europe," p. 22.

6. Andrei S. Markovits and Christopher Allen, "Trade Union and Economic Crisis: The West German Case," in Peter Gourevitch et al., eds., *Unions and Economic Crisis: Britain, West Germany, and Sweden* (London: George Allen & Unwin, 1984).

7. Ibid., pp. 96–97.

8. Evelyne Huber Stephens and John D. Stephens, "The Labor Movement, Political Power, and Workers' Participation in Western Europe," *Political Power and Social Theory* 3 (1982): 249; also, see Alfred Diamant, "Democratizing the Workplace: Myth and Reality in Mitbestimmung in the Federal Republic of Germany," paper delivered at the Annual Meeting of the American Political Science Association, 1976.

9. Markovits and Allen, "Trade Union and Economic Crisis," p. 163; and Diamant, "Industrial Democracy in Western Europe," p. 24.

10. Stephens and Stephens, "The Labor Movement," p. 232.

11. Friedrich Fulistenberg, "Workers' Participation in Management in the Federal Republic of Germany," *International Institute for Labour Studies*, Bulletin no. 6 (Geneva, 1973), p. 193.

12. Stephens and Stephens, "The Labor Movement," p. 133.

13. Diamant, "Myth and Reality in Mitbestimmung," p. 21.

14. *Workers' Participation*, Final Report of an International Management Seminar convened by the Organization for Economic Cooperation and Development, Versailles, March 5–8, 1975, p. 50.

15. Fulistenberg, "Workers' Participation in the Federal Republic of Germany," p. 193.

16. Christopher S. Allen, "Worker Participation and the German Trade Unions: An Unfulfilled Dream," in Sirianni, *Worker Participation*, p. 189.

17. Giuseppe Della Rocca, "Improving Participation: The Negotiation of New Technology in Italy and Europe," in Sirianni, *Worker Participation*, pp. 163–64.

18. *New York Times*, June 13, 1978, p. 24.

19. Stephens and Stephens, "The Labor Movement," p. 223.

20. Ibid., p. 234; Robert E. Cole, "The Macropolitics of Organizational Change: A Comparative Analysis of the Spread of Small-Group Activities," in Sirianni, *Worker Participation*, pp. 34–67.

21. Henry Milner, *Sweden: Social Democracy* (Oxford: Oxford University Press, 1989), p. 87.

22. Walter Korpi and Michael Shalev, "Strikes, Industrial Relations and Class Conflict in Capitalist Societies," *British Journal of Sociology* 30 (1979): 164–87.

23. Ibid., p. 172.

24. Cole, "The Macropolitics of Organizational Change," p. 43.

25. G. David Garson, *Worker Self-Management in Industry: European Experience* (New York: Praeger, 1977), p. 215.

26. M. Donald Hancock, "Productivity, Welfare and Participation in Sweden and West Germany," *Comparative Politics* (1978): 18.

27. Andrew Martin, "Trade Unions in Sweden: Strategic Resources to Change and Crisis," in Gourevitch et al., eds., *Unions and Economic Crisis*, p. 362.

28. Milner, *Sweden*, p. 139.

29. Ibid., p. 261.

30. Ibid., p. 130.

31. Martin, "Trade Unions in Sweden," p. 274.

32. Leif Widen, *Trade Union Funds in Sweden* (Stockholm: Swedish Employers' Confederation, 1988), p. 5.

33. Ibid.; Milner, *Sweden*.

34. Milner, *Sweden*, p. 284.

35. Ibid., quotation on p. 136.

36. Ibid., pp. 130–38.

37. Ibid., p. 137.

38. Garson, *Worker Self-Management*, p. 10; Diamant, "Industrial De-

mocracy in Western Europe," pp. 45–46; Milner, *Sweden*, p. 143.

39. Stephens and Stephens, "The Labor Movement," p. 229.

40. Yves Delamotte, "Workers' Participation and Personnel Politics in France," *International Labour Review* 127 (1988): 225.

41. Stephens and Stephens, "The Labor Movement," p. 230; Delamotte, "Workers' Participation and Personnel Politics in France," pp. 220–21.

42. George Ross, "*Autogestion* Coming and Going: The Strange Saga of Workers' Control Movements in Modern France," in Sirianni, *Worker Participation*, p. 219.

43. Ibid., p. 206.

44. Stephen Borstein and Sapsin K. Fine, "Workers' Participation and Self Government in France," paper delivered at the Annual Meeting of the American Political Science Association, 1976, p. 2.

45. Ross, "*Autogestion* Coming and Going," p. 210.

46. Borstein and Fine, "Workers' Participation in France," p. 23.

47. Ross, "*Autogestion* Coming and Going," p. 215.

48. W. Rand Smith, "Nationalization for What? Capitalist Power and Public Enterprise in Mitterrand's France," *Politics and Society* 18 (1990): 77.

49. Ibid., p. 90.

50. Martin Slater, "Worker Councils in Italy: Past Developments and Future Prospects," in Garson, *Worker Self-Management*, p. 192.

51. Ibid., p. 218.

52. Organization for Economic Cooperation and Development, *Workers' Participation*, Final Report (Versailles, 1975).

53. Ibid., p. 24.

54. *Economist*, Jan. 27, 1979, p. 34.

55. Joseph La Palombara, *Democracy Italian Style* (New Haven, Conn.: Yale University Press, 1987), p. 42.

56. Rocca, "Improving Participation," p. 14.

57. Stephens and Stephens, "The Labor Movement," p. 241.

58. Tiziano Treu and Serafino Negrelli, "Workers' Participation and Personnel Management Policy in Italy," *International Labour Review* 125 (1987): 943; also see Frederic Spotts and Theodore Wieser, *Italy: A Different Democracy* (London: Cambridge University Press, 1986).

59. J. H. Goldthorpe, "Industrial Reactions in Great Britain: A Cri-

tique of Reformism," in Tom Clarke and Laurie Clements, eds., *Trade Unions under Capitalism* (Atlantic Highlands, N.J.: Humanities Press, 1977).

60. Andre Gorz, *The Division of Labour* (Atlantic Highlands, N.J.: Humanities Press, 1976), p. 332.

61. *New York Times*, June 25, 1979, p. 25.

62. Tom Clarke, "Industrial Democracy: The Institutionalized Suppression of Industrial Conflict?" in Clarke and Clements, *Trade Unions under Capitalism*.

63. Alan Fox, "The Myth of Pluralism and a Radical Alternative," in Clarke and Clements, *Trade Unions under Capitalism*, pp. 145–46; Diamant, "Industrial Democracy in Western Europe," pp. 20–21.

64. Quoted in Jean Monds, "Workers' Control and the Historians: A New Economism," *New Left Review* 57 (1976): 17.

65. Clarke, "Industrial Democracy," p. 372.

66. Quoted in Peter Brannen, *Authority and Participation in Industry* (New York: St. Martin's Press, 1983), p. 58.

67. Ibid., pp. 101–2.

68. Ibid., p. 114.

69. Gourevitch et al., eds., *Unions and Economic Crisis*.

70. Anthony Borden, "Unraveling Union Ties, Labour Goes for the Vote," *In These Times*, June 20–July 3, 1990, p. 3.

71. Ibid.

72. Susan L. Woodward, "Freedom of the People Is in Its Private Life: The Unrevolutionary Implications of Industrial Democracy," *American Behavioral Scientist* 20 (1977): 284–85.

73. Fox, "The Myth of Pluralism," p. 143. Also see Tom Baumgartner, "Work, Politics, and Social Structure under Capitalism," in Tom R. Burns, Lars Erik Karlsson, and Veljko Rus, eds., *Work and Power*, Sage Studies in International Sociology, vol. 18 (Beverly Hills, Calif.: Sage Publications, 1979), p. 219.

Chapter 5

1. *New York Times*, July 2, 1979, p. B10.

2. Robert Drago and Terry McDonough, "Capitalist Shopfloor Initia-

tives, Restructuring, and Organizing in the 1980s," *Review of Radical Political Economics* 16 (1984): 52.

3. Ibid., p. 51.

4. Carmen Sirianni, "Worker Participation in the Late Twentieth Century: Some Critical Issues," in Carmen Sirianni, ed., *Worker Participation and the Politics of Reform* (Philadelphia: Temple University Press, 1987), p. 5.

5. Charles Heckscher, *The New Unionism: Employee Involvement in the Changing Corporation* (New York: Basic Books, 1988), p. 129.

6. Richard Edwards, *Contested Terrain: The Transformation of the Workplace in the Twentieth Century* (New York: Basic Books, 1979).

7. Charles Derber and William Schwartz, "Toward a Theory of Worker Participation," *Sociological Inquiry* 53 (1983): 83.

8. Patrick Michael Rooney, "Worker Participation in Employee-Owned Firms," *Journal of Economic Issues* 22 (June 1988): 456.

9. Derber and Schwartz, "Toward a Theory of Worker Participation," p. 66.

10. Rooney, "Worker Participation in Employee-Owned Firms," p. 451.

11. Arthur Hochner and Judith Goode et al., *Worker Buyouts and QWL* (Kalamozoo, Mich.: Upjohn Institute, 1988), p. 12.

12. Rooney, "Worker Participation in Employee-Owned Firms," p. 452.

13. Joseph Blasi, *Employee Ownership: Revolution or Ripoff?* (New York: Ballinger, 1988), p. 210.

14. Robert Kuttner, "Unions, Economic Power and the State," *Dissent* 32 (Winter 1986): 173.

15. Rooney, "Worker Participation in Employee-Owned Firms," p. 456; Hochner and Goode, *Worker Buyouts and QWL*, p. 271.

16. John Witte, *Democracy, Authority, and Alienation in Work* (Chicago: University of Chicago Press, 1980), p. 167.

17. Heckscher, *The New Unionism*, p. 130; Robert E. Cole, "The Macropolitics of Organizational Change," in Sirianni, *Worker Participation*, pp. 51–53.

18. Heckscher, *The New Unionism*, p. 130.

19. Ibid., p. 131.

20. Ibid., pp. 129–30.

186 *Notes*

21. Kuttner, "Unions, Economic Power and the State," p. 28.

22. Mike Parker, *Inside the Circle: A Union Guide to QWL* (Boston: South End Press, 1988); Sirianni, "Worker Participation," p. 15.

23. Thomas Kochan and Harry Katz et al., *Worker Participation and American Unions* (Kalamozoo, Mich.: Upjohn Institute, 1984), pp. 200–202.

24. Witte, *Democracy, Authority, and Alienation in Work*, pp. 25–26.

25. Derber and Schwartz, "Toward a Theory of Worker Participation," p. 69.

26. Witte, *Democracy, Authority, and Alienation in Work*, p. 26; Heckscher, *The New Unionism*, pp. 129–31; G. David Garson, "Automobile Workers and the Radical Dream," *Politics and Society* 3 (1973): 176.

27. Bennett Harrison and Barry Bluestone, *The Great U-Turn: Corporate Restructuring and the Polarization of America* (New York: Basic Books, 1988), p. 185.

28. Sirianni, "Worker Participation," p. 11.

29. Heckscher, *The New Unionism*, p. 28; Sirianni, "Worker Participation," p. 17.

30. Kochan and Katz, *Worker Participation and American Unions*, p. 128.

31. Quoted in Heckscher, *The New Unionism*, p. 28.

32. An exception is Glenn Watts, president of the Communication Workers of America, who believes that worker disillusionment with QWL and other programs results "from the fact that QWL often remains isolated within the organization as a whole." He advocates extending QWL to all levels of the organization. "I believe that for QWL to be effective in the long run, it must become not just a worker 'program,' but a part of values and relationships at all levels. We in CWA have recently taken our commitment to QWL a step further by starting the process within our own staff." Quoted in Kochan and Katz, *Worker Participation and American Unions*, p. 198.

33. For a similar view, see Heckscher, *The New Unionism*, and Kochan and Katz, *Worker Participation and American Unions*.

Chapter 6

1. Among the more recent works that favor workplace democracy are Benjamin Barber, *Strong Democracy: Participatory Democracy for a New Age* (Berkeley: University of California Press, 1985); Samuel

Bowles and Herbert Gintis, *Democracy and Capitalism: Property, Community, and the Contradictions of Social Thought* (New York: Basic Books, 1986); Martin Carnoy and Derek Shearer, *Economic Democracy: Challenge of the 1980s* (New York: M. E. Sharpe, 1979); Joshua Cohen and Joel Rogers, *On Democracy: Toward a Transformation of American Society* (London: Penguin, 1983); Robert Dahl, *A Preface to Economic Democracy* (Berkeley: University of California Press, 1985); Carol C. Gould, *Rethinking Democracy* (Cambridge: Cambridge University Press, 1988); Edward Greenberg, *Workplace Democracy: The Political Effects of Participation* (Ithaca, N.Y.: Cornell University Press, 1986); Christopher E. Gunn, *Workers' Self-Management in the United States* (Ithaca, N.Y.: Cornell University Press, 1984); Robert Lane, "From Political to Industrial Democracy," *Polity* 17 (1985): 623–48; and Ronald Mason, *Participatory and Workplace Democracy: A Theoretical Development in Critique of Liberalism* (Carbondale: Southern Illinois University Press, 1982).

2. Robert Dahl, *A Preface to Economic Democracy*, p. 135.

3. Ibid., p. 159.

4. Barber, *Strong Democracy*, p. 264.

5. Carole Pateman, *Participation and Democratic Theory* (Cambridge: Cambridge University Press, 1970), pp. 51, 72.

6. Ibid., 70.

7. Michael Poole, *Theories of Trade Unionism* (London: Routledge & Kegan Paul, 1981).

8. Quoted in Bryan David Wilson, *Ownership and Participation: The Politics of Employee Buyouts in the United States* (New Brunswick, N.J.: Rutgers University Press, 1985), p. 53.

9. Ibid., p. 57.

10. Edward Greenberg, "Industrial Self-Management and Political Attitudes," *American Political Science Review* 75 (1981): 29–42.

11. Ibid., p. 35.

12. Ibid., p. 40.

13. Ibid., p. 41.

14. Greenberg, *Workplace Democracy*, p. 171.

15. Greenberg, "Industrial Self-Management," p. 32.

Chapter 7

1. Robert Dahl, *After the Revolution* (New Haven, Conn.: Yale University Press, 1970), p. 46.

2. John Dewey, *The Public and Its Problems*, quoted in S. I. Benn and G. F. Gaus, eds., *Public and Private in Social Life* (New York: St. Martin's Press, 1983).

3. David Easton, *The Political System* (New York: Alfred A. Knopf, 1971), p. 134.

4. Christian Bay, for example, defines "as *political* all activities aimed at improving or protecting conditions for the satisfaction of human needs." He defines *pseudo-politics* as "activity that . . . is concerned with . . . promoting private or private interest-group advantage." Christian Bay, "Politics and Pseudopolitics: A Critical Evaluation of Some Behavioral Literature," *American Political Science Review* 59 (March 1965): 41. In a similar fashion, Benjamin Barber writes, "One can understand the realm of politics as being circumscribed by conditions that impose *a necessity for public action, and thus for reasonable public choice, in the presence of conflict and in the absence of private or independent grounds for judgment*." Benjamin Barber, *Strong Democracy: Participatory Democracy for a New Age* (Berkeley: University of California Press, 1984), p. 120.

5. Sheldon Wolin, *Politics and Vision* (Boston: Little, Brown, 1960), p. 434.

6. Hannah Arendt, *The Human Condition* (Chicago: University of Chicago Press, 1958), p. 203.

7. Hannah Arendt, *On Revolution* (New York: Viking Press, 1963), p. 120.

8. Ibid., p. 156.

9. Wolin, *Politics and Vision*, p. 433.

10. Ibid., p. 431.

11. Arendt, *On Revolution*, p. 273.

12. Wolin, *Politics and Vision*, pp. 429–34.

13. Arendt, *On Revolution*, p. 283.

14. Arendt, *The Human Condition*, pp. 29, 40, 203; Arendt, *On Revolution*, pp. 177–78; Wolin, *Politics and Vision*, p. 453.

15. Wolin, *Politics and Vision*, chap. 10. We have summarized Wolin's views as these were presented in 1960. His more recent articles and editorials in the now defunct journal *democracy* suggests that he has

moved much closer to what we are calling the participationist position. This position is articulated very forcefully in Wolin's magnificent new book, *The Presence of the Past* (Baltimore: Johns Hopkins University Press, 1989).

16. Carole Pateman, *The Disorder of Women: Democracy, Feminism, and Political Theory* (Stanford, Calif.: Stanford University Press, 1989), pp. 90–118; Ronald Mason, *Participatory and Workplace Democracy: A Theoretical Development in Critique of Liberalism* (Carbondale: Southern Illinois University Press, 1982), pp. 3–11.

17. Pateman, *The Disorder of Women*, pp. 90–118; Carole Pateman, *The Problem of Political Obligation* (New York: John Wiley & Sons, 1979), pp. 173–78; Robert Dahl, *A Preface to Economic Democracy* (Berkeley: University of California Press, 1985), pp. 91–110.

18. Marx's conception of the public, which is similar to Pateman's, makes the same error. See his "On the Jewish Question" in L. D. Easton and K. H. Guddat, eds., *Writings of the Young Marx on Philosophy and Society* (New York: Doubleday, 1967), pp. 216–48.

19. F. M. Barnard and R. A. Vernon, "Pluralism, Participation, and Politics," *Politics and Society* 3 (1975).

20. Carole Pateman, *Participation and Democratic Theory* (Cambridge: Cambridge University Press, 1970), pp. 42–43; Mason, *Participatory and Workplace Democracy*, p. 29; Barber, *Strong Democracy*, pp. 151, 232; C. B. Macpherson, *The Life and Times of Liberal Democracy* (Oxford: Oxford University Press, 1976), pp. 99–104.

21. Mason, *Participatory and Workplace Democracy*, p. 39.

22. Barber, *Strong Democracy*, p. 151.

23. Pateman, *The Disorder of Women*, pp. 118–40, 210–25.

24. Ibid., p. 135.

25. Ibid., p. 132.

26. John Stuart Mill, "The Subjection of Women," in Alice S. Rossi, ed., *Essays on Sex Equality* (Chicago: University of Chicago Press, 1970).

27. Pateman, *The Disorder of Women*, p. 130.

28. Ibid., p. 136.

29. Habermas in important respects serves as a precursor for an adequate participatory theory of the public (Jürgen Habermas, "The Public Sphere," *New German Critique* 6 [1974]: 49–55; Jürgen Habermas, *The Structural Transformation of the Public Sphere*, trans. Thomas Burger [Cambridge, Mass.: MIT Press, 1989]). The idea of the public sphere, according to Habermas, "calls for a rationalization of power

through the medium of public discussion among private individuals" (Habermas, "The Public Sphere," p. 55). With the complex inter-twining of the public and private realms that characterizes the later generations of modernity, we are witnessing a "'refeudalization' of the public sphere" (ibid., p. 54). Not only do political authorities actively regulate the economy but "social powers" such as large cor-porations assume political functions. Large organizations strive for an appearance of openness in order to preserve and enhance their legitimacy, but in reality they circumvent the public sphere wherever possible and work toward compromises with each other and with the state. "The idea of the public [thus] threatens to disintegrate with the structural transformation of the public sphere itself" (ibid., p. 55). Habermas believes that the public sphere can be preserved today only through the expansion of participatory democracy, con-strued as involving an equal power in decision making shared by the members of individual organizations. Habermas thus aligns him-self with a radical participationist position, emphasizing the need for the equalization of decision-making power among participants in as many forums of "private" decision making as possible to counteract the effects of the privatization of an expanded public sphere and the resultant circumvention of public accountability. If the feudalization of the public sphere is to be counteracted effectively, multiple arenas of decision making within the private sphere have to be reclassified as public space and thus rendered amenable to requirements of demo-cratic accountability and decision making. However, Habermas, like other participatory theorists, including Pateman, does not allow in his theory for adequate private space as a refuge against public inter-vention that would enable individuals and groups to develop and promote new ideas.

30. Dewey, *The Public and Its Problems* (Chicago: Swallow Press, 1954).

Chapter 8

1. Alexander Hamilton, John Jay, and James Madison, *The Federalist: A Commentary on the Constitution of the United States, Being a Collection of Essays Written in Support of the Constitution Agreed upon September 17, 1787 by the Federal Convention from the Original Text of Alexander Hamil-ton, John Jay and James Madison*, with an introduction by Edward Mead Earle (New York: Modern Library, 1941), p. 56.

2. Ibid., p. 55.

3. Ibid., p. 56.

4. Ibid., p. 57.

5. Ibid., p. 56.

6. Ibid., p. 55.

7. Ibid., p. 58.

8. Ibid., p. 61.

9. Martin Diamond, "Democracy and the Federalist: A Reconstruction of the Framers' Intent," *American Political Science Review* 53 (March 1959): 52–68.

10. Madison, *The Federalist*, No. 10, p. 59.

11. Ibid., No. 35, pp. 214–15.

12. Ibid., No. 10, p. 61.

13. Ibid., p. 62. "So deeply did Madison distrust state legislatures," writes William Riker, "that, throughout the Convention, he pushed for a national negative on state laws (see, especially, I, 164, 169; II, 27, 589, *The Papers of James Madison* (R. A. Rutland et al., eds., University of Chicago Press, 1962) and, afterward, writing to Jefferson, he described the Constitution pessimistically because it did not include the negative (Hobson, C. F., 'The Negative on State Laws: James Madison, the Constitution, and the Crisis of Republican Government,' *William and Mary Quarterly*, 1979, 36, 215–255)." William Riker, "The Heresthetics of Constitution-Making: The Presidency in 1787, with Comments on Determinism and Rational Choice," *American Political Science Review* 78 (March 1984): 3–4.

14. Madison, *The Federalist*, No. 35, p. 262.

15. Samuel Huntington, *American Politics: The Promise of Disharmony* (Cambridge, Mass.: Harvard University Press, 1981), p. 8.

16. In the 1790s Madison regarded the rise of the Federalist party as a fundamental threat to republican union. In 1792 he wrote that members of this party consisted of "those who . . . are more partial to the opulent than to the other classes of society; and having debauched themselves into a persuasion that mankind are incapable of governing themselves, it follows with them . . . that government can be carried on only by the pageantry of rank, the influence of money and emoluments, and the terror of military force." *The Writings of James Madison*, ed. Gailard Hunt (New York: G. P. Putnam's Son, 1900–1910), 6: 113–16. Quoted in Neil Riemer, *James Madison* (New York: Washington Square Press, 1968), p. 168.

17. Albert Hirschman, *The Passions and the Interests* (Princeton, N.J.: Princeton University Press, 1979).

18. John Ehrenreich and Barbara Ehrenreich, "The New Left: A Case Study in Professional-Management Class Radicalism," *Radical American* 2 (May–June 1977): 7–31.

19. Cf. Nicos Poulantzas, *Classes in Contemporary Capitalism* (London: New Left Books, 1975); Erik Olin Wright, *Class, Crisis, and the State* (London: New Left Books, 1987).

20. Michael Mann, "Social Cohesion of Liberal Democracy," in Anthony Giddens and David Held, eds., *Class, Power, and Conflict* (Berkeley: University of California Press, 1982).

21. E. P. Thompson, *The Making of the English Working Class* (New York: Vintage Books, 1963), p. 9.

22. Adam Przeworski, *Capitalism and Social Democracy* (New York: Cambridge University Press, 1985), p. 192.

23. Reeve Vanneman and Lynn Weber Cannon, *The American Perception of Class* (Philadelphia: Temple University Press, 1987), pp. 11–12.

24. Quoted by Terkel in ibid., p. 267.

25. George Novack, ed., *Their Morals and Ours: Marxist vs. Liberal on Morality* (New York: Pathfinder Press, 1973), p. 48.

26. Ibid., p. 70.

27. J. Tussman, *Obligation and the Body Politics*, quoted in Hanna Pitkin, "Justice: On Relating Private and Public," *Political Theory* 9 (1981): 347.

Chapter 9

1. Antonio Gramsci, *Selections from the Prison Notebooks* (New York: International, 1971), p. 158.

2. Calvin F. Exoo, ed., *Democracy Upside Down: Public Opinion and Cultural Hegemony in the United States* (New York: Praeger, 1987).

3. James Kluegel and Eliot R. Smith, *Beliefs about Inequality: Americans' View of What Is and What Ought to Be* (New York: Aldine De Gruyler, 1986); Michael Mann, *Consciousness and Action among the Western Working Class* (London: Macmillan Press, 1973); and Richard Sennett and Jonathan Cobb, *The Hidden Injuries of Class* (New York: Vintage Books, 1973).

4. G. David Garson, "Automobile Workers and the Radical Dream," *Politics and Society* 3 (1973): 166.

5. Ibid., pp. 165, 168. Also, see Mann, *Consciousness and Action*; and Kluegel and Smith, *Beliefs about Inequality*.

6. Mann, *Consciousness and Action*, p. 39.

7. Garson, "Automobile Workers," p. 166. For an excellent discussion of the meaning of democratic pluralism—one that presents alternative value positions—see William E. Connolly, *Appearance and Reality* (New York: Cambridge University Press, 1983).

8. Jerome Skolnick, *The Politics of Protest* (Washington, D.C.: Government Printing Office, 1969).

9. Herbert Gintis, "Communications and Politics: Marxism and the 'Problem' of Liberal Democracy," *Socialist Review* 10 (1980): 189–232; and Samuel Bowles and Herbert Gintis, *Democracy and Capitalism: Property, Community, and the Contradictions of Social Thought* (New York: Basic Books, 1986).

10. Christopher Gunn, *Workers' Self-Management in the United States* (Ithaca, N.Y.: Cornell University Press, 1984), pp. 23–24.

11. Ibid., pp. 22–25.

12. Carter Szymanski, "A Critique and Extension of the PMC," in Pat Waler, ed., *Between Labor and Capital* (Boston: South End Press, 1979), pp. 49–57.

13. Bowles and Gintis, *Democracy and Capitalism*; Samuel Bowles and Herbert Gintis, "Democratic Demands and Radical Rights," *Socialist Review* 19 (1989): 68; Charles Heckscher, *The New Unionism: Employee Involvement in the Changing Corporation* (New York: Basic Books, 1988).

14. Bowles and Gintis, "Democratic Demands," p. 68.

Bibliography

Allen, Christopher S. "Worker Participation and the German Trade Unions: An Unfulfilled Dream?" In Carmen Sirianni, ed., *Worker Participation and the Politics of Reform*. Philadelphia: Temple University Press, 1987.

Arendt, Hannah. *The Human Condition*. Chicago: University of Chicago Press, 1958.

———. *On Revolution*. New York: Viking Press, 1963.

Bachrach, Peter. "Interest, Participation and Democratic Theory." In J. Roland Pennock and John Chapman, eds., *Participation in Politics*. New York: Lieber-Atherton Press, 1975.

———. *The Theory of Democratic Elitism*. Boston: Little, Brown, 1967.

Bachrach, Peter, and Morton S. Baratz. *Power and Poverty: Theory and Practice*. New York: Oxford University Press, 1970.

Balbus, Isaac. "The Concept of Interest in Politics." *Politics and Society* 1 (1971): 151–77.

Barber, Benjamin. "Command Performance." *Harper's Magazine* 250 (April 1975): 51–54.

———. *Strong Democracy: Participatory Democracy for a New Age*. Berkeley: University of California Press, 1984.

Barnard, F. M., and R. A. Vernon. "Pluralism, Participation, and Politics." *Politics and Society* 3 (1975): 180–97.

Baumgartner, Tom. "Work, Politics, and Social Structure under Capitalism." In Tom R. Burns, Lars Erik Karlsson, and Veljko Rus, eds., *Work and Power*. Sage Studies in International Sociology, vol. 18. Beverly Hills, Calif.: Sage Publications, 1979.

Bay, Christian. "Politics and Pseudopolitics: A Critical Evaluation of Some Behavioral Literature." *American Political Science Review* 59 (March 1965): 39–51.

Benn, S. I., and G. F. Gaus, eds. *Public and Private in Social Life.* New York: St. Martin's Press, 1983.

Benton, Ted. "Realism, Power and Objective Interests." In Keith Graham, ed., *Contemporary Political Philosophy.* New York: Cambridge University Press, 1982.

Blasi, Joseph. *Employee Ownership: Revolution or Ripoff?* New York: Ballinger, 1988.

Block, Fred. "The Ruling Class Does Not Rule." *Socialist Revolution* 7, no. 3 (1977): 6–28.

Borden, Anthony. "Unraveling Union Ties, Labour Goes for the Vote." *In These Times,* June 20–July 3, 1990, pp. 6–7.

Borstein, Stephen, and Sapsin K. Fine. "Workers' Participation and Self Government in France." Paper delivered at the Annual Meeting of the American Political Science Association, 1976.

Bowles, Samuel, and Herbert Gintis. *Democracy and Capitalism: Property, Community, and the Contradictions of Social Thought.* New York: Basic Books, 1986.

————. "Democratic Demands and Radical Rights." *Socialist Review* 19 (1989): 57–72.

Brannen, Peter. *Authority and Participation in Industry.* New York: St. Martin's Press, 1983.

Burnham, Walter Dean. "Why Americans Don't Vote." *New Republic,* May 9, 1988, pp. 30–34.

Burns, James. *Leadership.* New York: Harper & Row, 1978.

Burns, Tom R., Lars Erik Karlsson, and Veljko Rus, eds. *Work and Power.* Sage Studies in International Sociology, vol. 18. Beverly Hills, Calif.: Sage Publications, 1979.

Carnoy, Martin. *The State and Political Theory.* Princeton, N.J.: Princeton University Press, 1984.

Carnoy, Martin, and Derek Shearer. *Economic Democracy: Challenge of the 1980s.* New York: M. E. Sharpe, 1979.

Clarke, Tom. "Industrial Democracy: The Institutionalized Suppression of Industrial Conflict?" In Tom Clarke and Laurie Clements, eds., *Trade Unions under Capitalism.* Atlantic Highlands, N.J.: Humanities Press, 1977.

Cohen, Joshua, and Joel Rogers. *On Democracy: Toward a Transformation of American Society.* London: Penguin, 1983.

Cole, Robert E. "The Macropolitics of Organizational Change: A Comparative Analysis of the Spread of Small-Group Activities." In

Carmen Sirianni, ed., *Worker Participation and the Politics of Reform.* Philadelphia: Temple University Press, 1987.

Coleman, James S. *Community Conflict.* New York: Macmillan, 1957.

Connolly, William. *Appearance and Reality in Politics.* New York: Cambridge University Press, 1983.

————. "On Interests in Politics." *Politics and Society* 2 (1972): 459–77.

————. *The Terms of Political Discourse.* Princeton, N.J.: Princeton University Press, 1983.

Dahl, Robert. *After the Revolution.* New Haven, Conn.: Yale University Press, 1970.

————. "Concept of Power." *Behavioral Science* 2 (1957): 201–15.

————. *A Preface to Economic Democracy.* Berkeley: University of California Press, 1985.

————. *Who Governs? Democracy and Power in an American City.* New Haven, Conn.: Yale University Press, 1961.

Dahrendorf, Ralf. *Class and Class Conflict in Industrial Society.* Stanford, Calif.: Stanford University Press, 1959.

Dallmayr, Fred R. "Democracy and Post-Modernism." *Human Studies* 10 (1986): 143–70.

Delamotte, Yves. "Workers' Participation and Personnel Politics in France." *International Labour Review* 127 (1988): 221–41.

Derber, Charles, and William Schwartz. "Toward a Theory of Worker Participation." *Sociological Inquiry* 53 (1983): 61–78.

Dewey, John. *The Public and Its Problems.* Chicago: Swallow Press, 1954.

Diamant, Alfred. "Democratizing the Workplace: Myth and Reality in Mitbestimmung in the Federal Republic of Germany." Paper delivered at the Annual Meeting of the American Political Science Association, 1976.

————. "Industrial Democracy in Western Europe." Paper delivered at the Annual Meeting of the American Political Science Association, 1982.

Diamond, Martin. "Democracy and the Federalist: A Reconstruction of the Framers' Intent." *American Political Science Review* 53 (March 1959): 52–58.

Drago, Robert, and Terry McDonald. "Capitalist Shopfloor Initiatives, Restructuring, and Organizing in the 1980s." *Review of Radical Political Economics* 16 (1984).

DuBoff, R. B. "Long-Term Economic Growth: Trends, Triumphs, Paradoxes." Unpublished manuscript, 1988.

Dunn, John. "Democracy Unretrieved, or the Political Theory of Professor Macpherson." *British Journal of Political Science*, 4 (1974): 487–99.

Dye, Thomas, and Harmon Zeigler. *The Irony of Democracy.* Pacific Grove, Calif.: Brooks/Cole, 1987.

Easton, David. *The Political System.* New York: Alfred A. Knopf, 1971.

Edsall, Thomas. *The New Politics of Inequality.* New York: W. W. Norton, 1984.

Edwards, Richard. *Contested Terrain: The Transformation of the Workplace in the Twentieth Century.* New York: Basic Books, 1979.

Ehrenreich, John and Barbara Ehrenreich. "The New Left: A Case Study in Professional-Management Class Radicalism," *Radical American* 2 (May–June 1977): 7–31.

Elster, Jon. "Sour Grapes—Utilitarianism and the Genesis of Wants." In Amartya Sen and Bernard Williams, eds., *Utilitarianism and Beyond.* Cambridge: Cambridge University Press, 1983.

Exoo, Calvin F., ed. *Democracy Upside Down: Public Opinion and Cultural Hegemony in the United States.* New York: Praeger, 1987.

Foucault, Michel. *Power/Knowledge*, ed. Colin Gordon. New York: Pantheon Books, 1980.

Fox, Alan. "The Myth of Pluralism and a Radical Alternative." In Tom Clarke and Laurie Clements, eds., *Trade Unions under Capitalism.* Atlantic Highlands, N.J.: Humanities Press, 1977.

Fulistenberg, Friedrich. "Workers' Participation in Management in the Federal Republic of Germany." *International Institute for Labour Studies*, Bulletin no. 6. Geneva, 1973.

Galbraith, John Kenneth. *The New Industrial State*, 3d ed. Boston: Houghton, Mifflin, 1976.

Garson, G. David. "Automobile Workers and the Radical Dream." *Politics and Society* 3 (1973): 163–77.

————, ed. *Worker Self-Management in Industry: European Experience.* New York: Praeger, 1977.

Gaventa, John. *Power and Powerlessness: Quiescence and Rebellion in an Appalachian Valley.* Oxford: Oxford University Press, 1980.

Gintis, Herbert. "Communications and Politics: Marxism and the 'Problem' of Liberal Democracy." *Socialist Review* 10 (1980): 189–232.

Goldfield, Michael. "Worker Insurgency, Radical Organization, and the New Deal." *American Political Science Review* 84 (1990): 1298–1315.

Goldthorpe, J. H. "Industrial Reactions in Great Britain: A Critique of Reformism." In Tom Clarke and Laurie Clements, eds., *Trade Unions under Capitalism.* Atlantic Highlands, N.J.: Humanities Press, 1977.

Gorz, Andre. *The Division of Labour.* Atlantic Highlands, N.J.: Humanities Press, 1976.

———. "Workers' Control Is More Than Just That." In Jerry Hunnius et al., eds., *Workers Control.* New York: Vintage Books, 1973.

Gould, Carol C. *Rethinking Democracy.* Cambridge: Cambridge University Press, 1988.

Gourevitch, Peter et al., eds. *Unions and Economic Crisis: Britain, West Germany, and Sweden.* London: George Allen & Unwin, 1984.

Gramsci, Antonio. *Selections from the Prison Notebooks.* New York: International, 1971.

———. "Soviets in Italy." *New Left Review* 51 (Sept.–Oct. 1968): 28–58.

Greenberg, Edward. "Industrial Self-Management and Political Attitudes." *American Political Science Review* 75 (1981): 29–42.

———. *Workplace Democracy: The Political Effects of Participation.* Ithaca, N.Y.: Cornell University Press, 1986.

Gunn, Christopher. *Workers' Self-Management in the United States.* Ithaca, N.Y.: Cornell University Press, 1984.

Gutmann, Amy. *Liberal Equality.* New York: Cambridge University Press, 1980.

Habermas, Jürgen. "The Public Sphere." *New German Critique* 6 (1974): 45–55.

———. *The Structural Transformation of the Public Sphere,* trans. Thomas Burger. Cambridge, Mass.: MIT Press, 1989.

Hamilton, Alexander, John Jay, and James Madison. *The Federalist: A Commentary on the Constitution of the United States, Being a Collection of Essays Written in Support of the Constitution Agreed upon September 17, 1787 by the Federal Convention from the Original Text of Alexander Hamilton, John Jay and James Madison,* with an introduction by Edward Mead Earle. New York: Modern Library, 1941.

Hancock, M. Donald. "Productivity, Welfare and Participation in Sweden and West Germany." *Comparative Politics* (1978): 4–23.

Harrison, Bennett, and Barry Bluestone. *The Great U-Turn: Corporate Restructuring and the Polarization of America.* New York: Basic Books, 1988.

Hayes, Edward. *Power Structure and Urban Policy.* New York: McGraw-Hill, 1972.

Heckscher, Charles. *The New Unionism: Employee Involvement in the Changing Corporation.* New York: Basic Books, 1988.

Hochner, Arthur, and Judith Goode et al. *Worker Buyouts and QWL.* Kalamozoo, Mich.: Upjohn Institute, 1988.

Hochschild, Jennifer. *The New American Dilemma.* New Haven, Conn.: Yale University Press, 1984.

Howe, Irving, ed. *Beyond the Welfare State.* New York: Schocken Books, 1982.

Hunt, Gailard, ed. *The Writings of James Madison.* New York: G. P. Putnam's Son, 1900–1910.

Huntington, Samuel. *American Politics: The Promise of Disharmony.* Cambridge, Mass.: Harvard University Press, 1981.

———. "United States." In Michael Crozier et al., eds., *Crisis of Democracy.* New York: New York University Press, 1976.

Kateb, George. "The Moral Distinctiveness of Representative Democracy." *Ethics* 91 (1981): 357–74.

Kaviraj, Sudipta. "Determination." Unpublished paper, New Delhi, 1989.

Keim, Donald W. "Participation in Contemporary Democratic Theories." In J. Roland Pennock and John W. Chapman, eds., *Participation in Politics.* New York: Lieber-Atherton, 1975.

Kluegel, James, and Eliot R. Smith. *Beliefs about Inequality: Americans' View of What Is and What Ought to Be.* New York: Aldine De Gruyler, 1986.

Kochan, Thomas, and Harry Katz et al. *Worker Participation and American Unions.* Kalamozoo, Mich.: Upjohn Institute, 1984.

Korpi, Walter, and Michael Shalev. "Strikes, Industrial Relations and Class Conflict in Capitalist Societies." *British Journal of Sociology* 30 (1979): 164–87.

Kuttner, Robert. "Unions, Economic Power and the State." *Dissent* 32 (Winter 1986): 167–75.

Lane, Robert. "From Political to Industrial Democracy." *Polity* 17 (1985): 623–48.

La Palombara, Joseph. *Democracy Italian Style.* New Haven, Conn.: Yale University Press, 1987.

Lindblom, Charles. "Another State of Mind: APSA Presidential Address." *American Political Science Review* 76 March (1982): 9–21.

———. *Politics and Markets: The World's Political Economic Systems.* New York: Basic Books, 1977.

Lipset, Seymour Martin. *Political Man.* Garden City, N.Y.: Doubleday, 1963.

Lukes, Steven. *Power: A Radical View.* London: Macmillan Press, 1974.

———. "The Real and Ideal World of Democracy." In Alkis Kantos, ed., *Power, Possessions and Freedom.* Toronto: University of Toronto Press, 1979.

McClosky, Herbert. "Consensus and Ideology in American Politics." *American Political Science Review* 58 (1964): 61–82.

McConnell, Grant. *Private Power and American Democracy.* New York: Alfred A. Knopf, 1967.

Macpherson, C. B. *Democratic Theory.* London: Oxford University Press, 1973.

———. *The Life and Times of Liberal Democracy.* Oxford: Oxford University Press, 1976.

Mann, Michael. *Consciousness and Action among the Western Working Class.* London: Macmillan Press, 1973.

———. "Social Cohension of Liberal Democracy." In Anthony Giddens and David Held, eds., *Class, Power, and Conflict.* Berkeley: University of California Press, 1982.

Markovits, Andrei S., and Christopher Allen. "Trade Union and Economic Crisis: The West German Case." In Peter Gourevitch et al., eds., *Unions and Economic Crisis: Britain, West Germany, and Sweden.* London: George Allen & Unwin.

Martin, Andrew. "Trade Unions in Sweden: Strategic Resources to Change and Crisis." In Peter Gourevitch et al., eds., *Unions and Economic Crisis: Britain, West Germany, and Sweden.* London: George Allen and Unwin, 1984.

Marx, Karl. "On the Jewish Question." In L. D. Easton and K. H. Guddat, eds., *Writings of the Young Marx on Philosophy and Society.* New York: Doubleday, 1967.

Mason, Ronald. *Participatory and Workplace Democracy: A Theoretical Development in Critique of Liberalism.* Carbondale: Southern Illinois University Press, 1982.

Mill, John Stuart. "The Subjection of Women." In Alice S. Rossi, ed., *Essays on Sex Equality.* Chicago: University of Chicago Press, 1970.

Miller, Richard. *Analyzing Marx: Morality, Power, and History*. Princeton, N.J.: Princeton University Press. 1984.

Milner, Henry. *Sweden: Social Democracy*. Oxford: Oxford University Press, 1989.

Monds, Jean. "Workers' Control and the Historians: A New Economism." *New Left Review* 97 (1976): 81–100.

Nagel, Jack. *Participation*. Englewood Cliffs, N.J.: Prentice Hall, 1987.

Novack, George, ed. *Their Morals and Ours: Marxist vs. Liberal on Morality*. New York: Pathfinder Press, 1973.

O'Connor, James. *The Fiscal Crisis of the State*. New York: St. Martin's Press, 1973.

Offe, Claus. *Contradictions of the Welfare State*. Cambridge, Mass.: MIT Press, 1984.

———. *Disorganized Capitalism*, ed. John Keane. Cambridge, Mass.: MIT Press, 1985.

Organization for Economic Cooperation and Development. *Workers' Participation*, Final Report of an International Management Seminar. Versailles, 1975.

Parenti, Michael. "Power and Pluralism: A View from Below." *Journal of Politics* 32 (1970): 501–30.

Parker, Mike. *Inside the Circle: A Union Guide to QWL*. Boston: South End Press, 1988.

Pateman, Carole. *The Disorder of Women: Democracy, Feminism, and Political Theory*. Stanford, Calif.: Stanford University Press, 1989.

———. *Participation and Democratic Theory*. Cambridge: Cambridge University Press, 1970.

———. *The Problem of Political Obligation*. New York: John Wiley & Sons, 1979.

———. "Sublimation and Reification: Locke, Wolin, and the Liberal Democratic Conception of the Political." *Politics and Society* 5 (1975): 441–67.

Pennock, J. Roland. *Democratic Theory*. Princeton, N.J.: Princeton University Press, 1982.

Pennock, J. Roland, and John Chapman, eds. *Participation in Politics*. New York: Lieber-Atherton Press, 1975.

Peterson, Paul. *City Limits*. Chicago: University of Chicago Press, 1981.

Phillips, Kevin. *Politics of Rich and Poor*. New York: Random House, 1990.

Pitkin, Hanna. "Justice: On Relating Private and Public." *Political Theory* 9 (1981): 327–52.

————. *Representation*. New York: Atherton Press, 1969.

Piven, Frances Fox, and Richard Cloward. *Regulating the Poor: The Functions of Public Welfare*. New York: Pantheon Books, 1971.

Polsby, Nelson W. *Community Power and Political Theory*. New Haven, Conn.: Yale University Press, 1963.

Poole, Michael. *Theories of Trade Unionism*. London: Routledge & Kegan Paul, 1981.

Poulantzas, Nicos. *Classes in Contemporary Capitalism*. London: New Left Books, 1975.

————. *Political Power and Social Classes*. London: N.L.B. and Sheed & Ward, 1973.

Przeworkski, Adam. *Capitalism and Social Democracy*. New York: Cambridge University Press, 1985.

Riemer, Neil. *James Madison*. New York: Washington Square Press, 1968.

Riker, William. "The Heresthetics of Constitution-Making: The Presidency in 1787, with Comments on Determinism and Rational Choice." *American Political Science Review* 78 (March 1984): 1–17.

Rocca, Giuseppe Della. "Improving Participation: The Negotiation of New Technology in Italy and Europe." In Carmen Sirianni, ed., *Worker Participation and the Politics of Reform*. Philadelphia: Temple University Press, 1987.

Rooney, Patrick Michael. "Worker Participation in Employee-Owned Firms." *Journal of Economic Issues* 22 (June 1988): 451–58.

Rose, Stephen J. *The American Profile Poster: Who Owns What*. New York: Pantheon, 1986.

Ross, George. "*Autogestion* Coming and Going: The Strange Saga of Workers' Control Movements in Modern France." In Carmen Sirianni, ed., *Worker Participation and the Politics of Reform*. Philadelphia: Temple University Press, 1987.

Rutland, R. A. et al., eds. *The Papers of James Madison*. Chicago: University of Chicago Press, 1962.

Schaar, John. "Legitimacy in the Modern State." In Phillip Green and Sanford Levinson, eds., *Power and Community*. New York: Pantheon Books, 1970.

Schattschneider, E. E. *The Semi-Sovereign People: A Realist's View of Democracy in America.* New York: Holt, Rinehart and Winston, 1960.

Sennett, Richard, and Jonathan Cobb. *The Hidden Injuries of Class.* New York: Vintage Books, 1973.

Sirianni, Carmen. "Worker Participation in the Late Twentieth Century: Some Critical Issues." In Carmen Sirianni, ed., *Worker Participation and the Politics of Reform.* Philadelphia: Temple University Press, 1987.

Skocpol, Theda, and Kenneth Finegold. "Explaining New Deal Labor Policy." *American Political Science Review* 84 (1990): 1297–1315.

Skolnick, Jerome. *The Politics of Protest.* Washington, D.C.: Government Printing Office, 1969.

Slater, Martin. "Worker Councils in Italy: Past Developments and Future Prospects." In G. David Garson, ed., *Worker Self-Management in Industry: European Experience.* New York: Praeger, 1977.

Smith, W. Rand. "Nationalization for What? Capitalist Power and Public Enterprise in Mitterrand's France." *Politics and Society* 18 (1990): 75–101.

Spotts, Frederic, and Theodore Wieser. *Italy: A Different Democracy.* London: Cambridge University Press, 1986.

Stephens, Evelyne Huber, and John D. Stephens. "The Labor Movement, Political Power, and Workers' Participation in Western Europe." *Political Power and Social Theory* 3 (1982): 215–49.

Stone, Clarence. *Economic Growth and Neighborhood Discontent.* Chapel Hill: University of North California Press, 1976.

———. "Systemic Power in Community Decision Making." *American Political Science Review* 74 (December 1980): 978–90.

Susser, Ida. *Norman Street: Poverty and Politics in an Urban Neighborhood.* New York: Oxford University Press, 1982.

Szymanski, Carter. "A Critique and Extension of the PMC." In Pat Waler, ed., *Between Labor and Capital.* Boston: South End Press, 1979.

Thompson, E. P. *The Making of the English Working Class.* New York: Vintage Books, 1963.

Treu, Tiziano, and Serafino Negrelli. "Workers' Participation and Personnel Management Policy in Italy." *International Labour Review* 126 (1987): 81–94.

Tzu, Lao. *The Way of Life.* New York: Perigee Books, 1980.

Vanneman, Reeve, and Lynn Weber Cannon. *The American Perception of Class*. Philadelphia: Temple University Press, 1987.

Verba, Sidney, and Norman Nie. *Participation in America: Political Democracy and Social Equality*. New York: Harper & Row, 1972.

Wall, Grenville. "The Concept of Interest in Politics." *Politics and Society* 5 (1975): 487–510.

Wicker, Tom. "The Holes in the Economy." *New York Times*, September 2, 1988.

Widen, Leif. *Trade Union Funds in Sweden*. Stockholm: Swedish Employers' Confederation, 1988.

Wilson, Bryan David. *Ownership and Participation: The Politics of Employee Buyouts in the United States*. New Brunswick, N.J.: Rutgers University Press, 1985.

Witte, John. *Democracy, Authority, and Alienation in Work*. Chicago: University of Chicago Press, 1980.

Wolin, Sheldon. *Politics and Vision*. Boston: Little, Brown, 1960.

———. *The Presence of the Past*. Baltimore, Johns Hopkins University Press, 1989.

Woodward, Susan L. "Freedom of the People Is in Its Private Life: The Unrevolutionary Implications of Industrial Democracy." *American Behavioral Scientist* 20 (1977): 279–96.

Wright, Erik Olin. *Class, Crisis, and the State*. London: New Left Books, 1987.

Index